ENERGY OPTIONS

*An introduction to small-scale
renewable energy technologies*

Edited and introduced by
DRUMMOND HISLOP

INTERMEDIATE TECHNOLOGY PUBLICATIONS 1992

Intermediate Technology Publications Ltd
103–105 Southampton Row, London WC1B 4HH, UK

© Intermediate Technology Publications 1992

British Library Cataloguing-in-Publication Data

Energy options: An introduction to small-scale
renewable energy technologies.
    I. IT Power
    333.79

    ISBN 1–85339–082–8

The photos on pp. 11, 49, 61, 75, 84, 86, 96 are courtesy of Peter Fraenkel.
Typeset by Inforum Typesetting, Portsmouth
Printed by SRP Exeter

Contents

Preface

World events, political, economic and environmental, have brought about periodic resurgences of interest in 'alternative' sources of energy. Much of the interest has been born of panic and has been short-lived as conflicts have been resolved and economic changes accommodated. For those of us more involved with the problems of developing countries than with temporary Western whims, the energy question does not go away and many people have been working, continuously, to perfect methods of energy provision for those without access to fossil fuel sources of power. The products of their work will be regarded as 'alternative' but would be better thought of as 'renewable' resources.

This book is devoted to the options available in energy resources of a non-fossil nature. Its purpose is to explain what can and cannot be done, what realistically can be expected and, not least, to point out the potential problems, both practical and economic, which might have to be faced in using the various techniques and technologies.

Energy Options does not attempt to provide all the answers to all energy questions but gives a comprehensive overview of the options currently available. It is intended for those who need to know where, and how, they might be used but who have neither the time nor the facilities to research all the possibilities for themselves. With the information provided here, the potentially useful techniques for a given situation will be more easily identified for detailed investigation and, hopefully, successful application.

Energy Options has its roots in a series of leaflets initiated by the Intermediate Technology Development Group (ITDG) in the late 1970s to meet a need for informative summaries on a variety of technical subjects. The subjects themselves were defined by the technical enquiries received from people all over the world who looked, and still look, to ITDG as a source of information not easily found elsewhere. The leaflets were designed to meet the needs of different people in different ways. For the casually interested enquirer, they provided enough information to satisfy initial curiosity. For the busy decision-maker, they offered a briefing on technical subjects without clouding the issue with too much detail. Thus, they became known as 'Technical Briefs'. For the worker required to implement the decisions, they provided a basic understanding of the technology and offered a springboard to further, serious research into the subject.

In many cases, they served merely to eliminate a technology from a reader's agenda – so saving valuable time and effort on futile research. Over the years, the Technical Brief has become a successful and useful tool and has been adopted as a product of the Technical Enquiry Unit, the focus of ITDG's technical information services. Each is prepared by a specialist in the subject – and often criticized by others – to ensure that accurate and up-to-date information is presented. As far as possible, any prices quoted are checked regularly and those given here were correct in July 1991.

For this volume, those Technical Briefs known in the Unit as the energy briefs have been updated and re-written to represent, if not the 'State of the Art', a serious presentation of the renewable energy options currently available. Not all will be options available to all readers, as will be obvious from the text, but the potential user of the techniques described should gain a sufficient understanding to be able to make some preliminary decisions and to follow these up with a more detailed investigation.

It should be recorded with thanks that the original Technical Briefs on which this book is based were prepared for the Technical Enquiry Unit by, in particular, Bernard McNelis, Peter Fraenkel and Tony Derrick of IT Power; Drummond Hislop, Jeff Kenna and Gareth Jones of ESD; and Ray Holland, Andy Brown and Adam Harvey of ITDG.

Bob Spencer
Technical Enquiry Unit
ITDG
July 1991

1 Introduction

For most developing countries, interest in renewable energy technologies was originally a response to the energy shortages and price increases of the early and late 1970s. But by mid-1990, international oil prices were back to levels as low, in real terms, as they were in the late 1960s. In this context, it is instructive to reflect on why there is still interest in renewable energy technologies, what the contribution of renewable energies to developing countries has so far been, and what is likely to be their future contribution.

The increasing demand for energy

In almost all developing countries the demand for energy is growing as populations increase and as economic development takes place; a process which is often conventionally associated with increasing per capita consumption of energy.

But in most of these countries, it is all too clear that there are limits on the ability of existing energy resources and delivery systems to meet this increasing energy demand, especially in the energy forms needed by low-income groups and at prices they can afford. The situation varies both between and within countries, but some broadly valid observations on why this happens can still be made. In doing so it is useful to distinguish between two categories of energy resource and delivery systems – the traditional and the modern/conventional.

Traditional energy systems

The traditional energy resource base in developing countries is biomass (over 80 of total energy use in some of the poorest countries) in the form of wood, wood and crop residues, and animal residues. This biomass provides mainly heat for domestic cooking, space heating, and commercial and industrial heat processes, especially for processing agricultural and forestry products. Direct solar energy provides further heat for drying crops and animal products.

Energy in the form of draught power is also provided by biomass, although indirectly, in the form of food and fodder for animals and humans. Biomass as a source of power is also often supplemented by traditional water and wind technologies.

1

Over the past few decades, many developing countries have suffered rapid reductions in the capacity of traditional energy systems to supply the energy needs of their growing populations at existing levels of per capita consumption, let alone those associated with economic growth. There are many reasons for this, often inter-related, and combinations of the following are usually important:

○ Land clearances for agriculture, large-scale cash-cropping and monocultures, urban and industrial developments, hydro-electric, drainage and other infrastructural development, and the wind and water erosion and salination that so often follow them, can and often do reduce the biomass available as a direct energy resource.

○ Rapid urbanization, population increases and overgrazing all increase demand on biomass resources. In many cases demand goes beyond the capacity of the land to replace the biomass removed, leading to reductions in biomass stocks and production.

○ Armed conflict can have the same effect by forcing populations to move to areas unable to sustain them.

○ Restricted access to or ownership of land forces poor people to exploit biomass resources on what land to which they do have access to, unsustainably.

○ Some experts argue that climatic change also contributes to reductions in biomass cover in some parts of the world, especially in areas vulnerable to the expansion of existing deserts.

Conventional modern energy systems

For many years, the modern/conventional sector has gradually supplemented and replaced traditional energy resources. Liquid fossil fuels are used for static power (e.g. irrigation pumping, milling) and mobile power (e.g. for tractors and related machinery, and for transport); kerosene is used for lighting and for domestic cooking, and oil or gas for process heat. Finally, rural electrification, usually from fossil fuels or large scale hydro, has brought electricity for power, lighting, entertainment and refrigeration.

However, the ability of the conventional modern sector to meet all the energy demands of both increasing populations and increasing economic activity, especially in the rural areas, is also limited. In the case of domestic heat energy, although kerosene is usually available in urban areas, and often in rural areas, supplies are frequently interrupted. In rural areas, its costs are usually high relative to those of biomass fuels, so although it is used for lighting by most people, its use as a cooking fuel tends to be restricted to high-income groups. Cooking by liquid petroleum gas (LPG) or electricity is, in most rural areas, confined to very small minorities.

2

The purchasing power of industry allows it to overcome biomass fuel shortages more readily than households. Even so, in many countries rural and even urban industries who had switched to oil for heat have then been forced back onto wood because of rising fossil fuel costs.

In the case of power, diesel generators, engines and pumps are very common. But again, supplies of low-cost fuels are not necessarily secure, while operating costs can be very high. Many rural villages are electrified in the sense that the grid has reached them. But the proportion of households within the village which is actually connected is, in many areas, very low. This is largely because of connection costs; but it is also because low-income levels, and the lack of industrial customers mean that load factors on rural electrification schemes are very low, and tariffs are, unless subsidized, too high to be afforded by poor people.

Meanwhile, the costs of providing further rural electrification schemes increase, while the ability of many developing countries to afford the necessary foreign exchange is also limited. Large hydro-electric schemes run into increasing opposition on the grounds of population removal, deforestation and environmental considerations. Environmental and cost pressures also work against fossil and nuclear installations, and are likely to do so even more in the future.

In this context it is likely that scarce capital resources and foreign exchange will tend to be devoted to large-scale conventional schemes which serve urban areas and major industrial plant. Although conventional rural electrification in the form of grid extensions will continue, it is unlikely to meet more than a small fraction of the unmet power demand of many rural populations, especially those in isolated and/or mountainous areas.

The role of renewables

It is clear that there is a gap, both now and in the future, between the energy needs of economic development, especially in rural areas, and the ability of both the traditional and the conventional modern energy sectors to meet this need. In seeking means of bridging this gap, consumers, rural energy planners and decision-makers need to bear in mind what energy technologies will contribute to sustainable development. Here are five criteria for sustainable development, together with brief comments on the extent to which renewable energy technologies meet them:

○ They should be appropriate in ownership terms to local needs and resources. (Most renewable energy systems, apart from large and mini-hydro, are small-scale, stand-alone systems, amenable to local ownership and control.)

○ They should, as far as possible, generate income and employment in rural areas, and use minimal foreign exchange. (Some renewable technologies – e.g. micro-hydro, biogas – can be manufactured locally, at least in part, and thus reduce dependence on imported parts and fuels.)

○ They should have minimal negative impact on the productive capacity of the land: this means at worst avoiding, and at best reducing soil erosion from wind, water or salination. (Biomass-based and hydro systems can be environmentally harmful or beneficial, depending on, for example, the design of the overall production system – other renewable energy technologies are usually environmentally neutral or beneficial.)

○ They must take into account the fact that there is likely to be increasing pressure in future years for energy systems, even rural energy systems, in developing countries, to conform to stricter emission standards, such as that of CO_2. (Provided biomass systems are self-sustaining, all renewables meet this criterion.)

○ They should provide a secure supply of energy, which will not be interrupted by international crises. (Except insofar as imported spares are needed, all renewables meet this criterion.)

Clearly, renewable energy technologies have the potential to meet many of the criteria outlined above, and many commentators suggest that they should be promoted on a large scale in developing countries. The following section discusses some of the possibilities and problems in more detail.

What are the 'renewables'?

Renewable energy technologies are extremely varied in both type and scale, in the problems and opportunities that they present, and in the uses to which they can effectively be put. They can be categorized in different ways, which have different implications for their end uses and dissemination. One set of categories distinguishes between the new and unfamiliar, and the relatively familiar. At one extreme, solar photovoltaic (solar PV) is a completely new technology, which so far has had little impact in the industrialized countries, let alone in the developing world. Solar thermal and the production of liquid fuels from biomass (the latter is not covered in this book because it is a large-scale technology with limited relevance in the developing world at present) also fall in this category.

At the other extreme, many of the technologies are concerned with the combustion and consumption by humans and animals of biomass, which already provides the vast majority of the energy needed in many poor countries. These technologies – improved biomass kilns, stoves, ovens and furnaces; biogas and producer gas; steam and Stirling engines – together with micro-hydro and wind, consist of modernized versions of technologies from the nineteenth centry or even earlier, which provide cost and/or performance-related improvements over the traditional versions, and which, in many cases, make the technology much more widely available than was possible before.

In the first case, an emphasis on renewables implies the introduction of a completely new concept; in the latter, improvements in existing biomass production or conversion systems.

Another basic difference between the various renewable technologies is their product, the two categories being power and heat. The power technologies covered in this book are solar PV, micro-hydro, hydrams and wind, together with the four biomass power technologies – biogas, producer gas for power, and steam and Stirling engines. The heat technologies are solar thermal, solar distillation, solar drying, charcoal, producer gas for heat, stoves and industrial combustion.

The power categories can be divided further according to the scale of power produced in a typical installation, and to costs. Solar PV systems cost (although it is possible that in the future costs will fall) upwards of US$6000/kWe installed, and installed systems are rarely more than 1 to 2 kWpe. This contrasts with micro-hydro, and with producer gas as the main existing example of a biomass-fuelled power system. Their capital costs are in the region of US$1500 and US$350 to $1000/kWe installed, respectively. All these should be taken in the context of the capital costs of small diesel generators, which can be as low as US$150/kWe in countries such as Bangladesh and India.

Obviously, diesel and producer gas systems (and other biomass-fuelled power systems) have much higher operation and maintenance costs, and, above all, fuel costs. On a lifetime cost basis, these running costs must be added to their capital costs, countering at least some of their capital cost advantages with respect to technologies with higher per kW installed costs such as solar PV.

The impact of renewables

If we now look at the role of renewables in the developing countries so far, two basic points must be emphasised.

First, with the exception of ethanol in Brazil, Malawi and Zimbabwe, the renewable technologies have had no impact on liquid-fuelled transport systems, and are unlikely to do so in the near future. Second, the contribution of the improved and new renewable energy technologies described in this book (excluding large hydro systems) to static power or to improvements in fuel efficiency in heat systems is, so far, negligible. There are certainly a number of success stories – for example household stoves in Sri Lanka, micro-hydro in Nepal, biogas in Orissa and solar PV for household lighting in the Dominican Republic. These successes only serve however to highlight the many failures in the twenty years since support for the use of renewable energy technologies gained ground in the early 1970s.

5

There are many complex and inter-related reasons for this lack of impact, and it is important that they should be made clear if greater success in the dissemination of renewable energy technologies is to be achieved during the next decade. Four of the most important reasons are:

○ Very few of the renewable energy technologies so far promoted in developing countries are in widespread use in industrialized countries. This means that production volumes are low, costs tend to be high, and support systems (information, training, spares, maintenance) are not available, even in urban areas. In rural areas, where most of these technologies tend to be located, support systems may be even more difficult to establish.

○ In many cases, the technologies put into the field are unreliable prototypes produced by technical research organizations, with little understanding of the real needs of potential users and beneficiaries.

○ Although maintenance and the supply of fuel can be difficult problems in certain areas at different times, the small diesel engine is a remarkably cost-effective, long-life, well-supported, convenient, familiar and flexible means of providing power. This makes it extremely hard for competing power technologies to be established in the market.

○ Biomass power systems need to be integrated with the agriculture/ forestry sector. While this can provide very great economic and environmental benefits, it is difficult to establish the necessarily complex management and organizational systems.

○ Despite reductions in biomass availability, biomass fuel costs are still relatively low in most countries, and improving fuel efficiency may not be a high priority amongst fuel users. This makes the introduction of new combustion technologies more difficult; other potential benefits have however to be considered in the dissemination of these technologies, such as speed of cooking and reduction in smoke levels (improved domestic stoves), changes in the product quality (improved brick kilns).

Renewable power systems

The renewable technology that has probably received the greatest attention and promotion in developing countries from external sources and development agencies, is solar PV. In developing countries, solar PV has been promoted to provide very small amounts of high-value power for lighting, health clinics, pumping, vaccine refrigeration, communications, etc. Most solar PV projects provide less than 1kW of electricity, and in quantitative terms, the impact of solar PV has been minimal. Global PV sales are about 40MW/year, most of which is for items such as watches and

6

calculators. The developing countries' share of larger systems for power is not known, but is certainly not more than a few MW per year.

In contrast to the commercial status of solar PV, research on and dissemination of small-scale biomass power technologies – mainly producer gas – has taken place in the developing countries, without commercial backup or stimulus. The results have been piecemeal; although several hundred small systems have been installed, especially in Asia, technical viability is not yet assured, while the problems of support systems, especially on the fuel supply side and its integration with agricultural and forestry production, have hardly been addressed. Steam plant is limited to very small numbers of traditional large systems, and although over 100 small Stirling engines have been installed in the field in India, evaluation has not been made public, and it is not known whether or not the programme will continue.

Plant output for all these technologies is usually very much larger than that of PV systems – in the range of 5 to 50kWe for producer gas, suitable either for one specific power use such as milling, or for a village grid system. These higher outputs and the capital cost differences noted above, have important implications for energy technology choice, which will be discussed below.

Micro-hydro has been extremely successful in Nepal, with several hundred direct-drive milling systems of up to 25kW. Some of these installations have electricity generation as a secondary benefit, and now an increasing number of dedicated electricity generation systems are now being installed. In Sri Lanka the rehabilitation of micro-hydro of between 30 and 120kW on tea estates has been very successful. These successes could be replicated in the longer term in Peru, Zimbabwe, Ethiopia and Vietnam, amongst many other countries which have significant and suitable hydro potential.

Wind power has been less successful. Although there are thought to be 750000 windpumps in use throughout the world, most have been in Australia, the US, South Africa and Argentina, where they used designs too expensive for widespread use in developing countries. Over the past twenty years newer models using modern materials and design methods have been introduced. For example, over 200 Kijito windpumps have been produced by a Kenyan manufacturer, the project having been initiated with an ITDG design and ODA finance. Other windmills for both pumping and electricity generation on a very small scale, mainly produced locally, are in operation elsewhere in the developing world.

The number of installations however is still very small compared to the total power supply and demand. The deciding factors are windmill availability, windmill cost and the availability of suitable wind speeds. Windpumps may be competitive with diesel pumpsets in some places, provided the wind regime is favourable. But, unfortunately, global wind patterns mean that wind speeds in the tropics are, averaged over the year, lower than those in higher latitudes, so that wind generators – which need relatively high wind speeds to be cost-effective – may have only limited application in many developing countries.

Biogas has a very variable record. Much of the effort to disseminate community biogas systems has foundered on problems of payment for raw material collection and of distribution of the gas. Family-sized systems work well in some countries, such as India and Nepal, although it is not clear if this is possible without subsidies. Larger systems (e.g. pig farms) work well and can be economic.

Renewable heat sources

It is generally recognized that energy efficiency in the combustion of biomass fuels for household, commercial, institutional and industrial use is highly desirable on both economic and environmental grounds, and many projects have undertaken improvements in combustion systems. The results have been variable. In domestic stoves programmes, for example, the success rate has, until recently, been low. However, as the complexities of technology choice in the household context, and the methods of dealing with them, become more widely recognized, success is becoming more common. One of the most important developments has been the realization that improving energy performance may not be the most important benefit of an improved stove as far as the housewife is concerned; issues of health, safety, convenience and child care are often the primary consideration.

Relatively little work has been undertaken on improving biomass combustion systems for industry, except in the plantation industries such as tea, rubber and tobacco. The reasons for this are discussed in Chapter 6. Here is is enough to note that the scope for interventions to improve the performance of renewable energy systems is enormous, with important consequences both for the industrial unit concerned, and for the national economies of the developing nations as a whole.

Renewable versus non-renewable – some issues

The choice of an energy technology, whether between renewable and non-renewable, or between renewables, is often a complex issue. At one level, there is the simple question of whether or not the basic resource is available – whether there is sufficient wind, sun, water head and flow, etc. At another level, it is necessary to compare the costs of the various means available of providing the energy needed. But at a third level, it is also important to define precisely what energy needs exist in the community or plant, what priorities are to be set amongst them, and what funds are to be allocated to meet them. It is in this context that an inappropriate choice can be made, particularly between renewable and non-renewable technologies.

8

This sometimes happens when renewable energy projects are used to promote a particular technology, rather than as a means of using the most appropriate energy technology to solve a specific problem. In one example, PV pumps are supplied free for village water-supply programmes. Technically, the project works perfectly, and from the point of view of the recipient it is an appropriate choice of energy technology for pumping, as he or she does not have to bear the capital costs, and the running costs are very low indeed.

However, the installed costs of solar PV continue to be so high that the typical 1.3kWp array used to supply electricity to the pump are the same as the installed costs of between two and five 5kW diesel generators. Although their running costs are much higher, each of these generators could provide power not only for the water supply, but also for a wide range of uses such as irrigation, milling, lighting and entertainment, provided the fuel and maintenance support systems were in place. From the national point of view, or from the point of view of someone who has to purchase the technology, it has to be recognized that buying diesel generators might well be a more optimal use of the capital available, a very important consideration in countries where shortages of capital are serious constraints on economic development.

The lesson is that it is important not to isolate one power requirement from overall energy needs, without careful thought. Where very small amounts of high priority power are needed, such as for vaccine refrigeration, a high-cost power system such as solar PV may be appropriate. But in general, the overall energy context should be taken into account, and this may often result in a different choice, one which maximizes the benefits from the investment. In some case, the resulting choice will be a non-renewable rather than a renewable energy technology.

This is not to suggest that solar PV has no role to play; examples of its use for very low quantities of very high value power have already been cited, and where small amounts of capital are available to individuals, or can be made available, for example on rotating credit schems, it may well be rational to purchase very small PV systems for individual households lighting, to replace kerosene.

The benefit maximization approach leads on to a prediction for the future. If, as many Indian and other researchers on producer gas and Stirling systems suggest, reliable small biomass-fuelled power systems do soon become available, the production of fuels for them can add value to the products of improved multi-purpose biomass production systems. This will help to establish the wide range of benefits from more effective biomass production discussed in greater detail in Chapter 2, including soil stabilization, improvements in agricultural productivity and local income-creation.

To summarize then, it is clear that the renewable energy technologies do have an important role, although limited at the moment, to play in the energy economies of the developing countries. The extent of this role is likely to increase in the future, as technologies mature and reduce in cost, as support systems are established, and as linkages with other production sectors develop. However, it is important to recognize that inappropriate choice of high-cost renewables in capital-short conditions will provide, at best, very limited and probably only short-term benefits to the community. Moreover, such choices are likely to detract from the long-term growth of the market for renewable energies.

From this, two basic principles for the choice of energy systems in developing countries can be derived. First, in conditions of energy and capital shortage, only those energy technologies that are reliable, and that maximize the energy outputs needed by the community as a whole for the capital available should be adopted. Very small amounts of high-cost power from renewables will not always meet this condition, as the same and additional amounts of power can often be provided more economically by other means. The real need is for funding agencies to examine overall energy requirements in any particular area, and not to concentrate on the energy needs of one activity alone.

Second, it has to be recognized that as biomass is still the dominant energy resource, relatively marginal adjustments to biomass systems will tend to provide much larger benefits overall to the community than can the introduction of small amounts of energy from completely new or unfamiliar technologies. From this it is a logical step to suggest that in the long term, major improvements in the efficiency of biomass combustion systems of all sizes, together with the introduction of reliable small biomass-fuelled power systems, are likely to be the renewable technologies with the greatest impact in most developing countries. The full benefit of these technologies will only become available through the development of a much broader approach to energy systems, and to their links to land management and agricultural and forestry systems, than currently prevails.

But in the end, the decision-maker has to make his or her own informed choice. The chapters which form the body of this book are designed to help with these choices, but it is important to bear in mind three considerations which fall outside the technical issues discussed in them. The first is that renewable energy technologies are not always the most appropriate solution to an energy-supply problem; the second is that, as far as possible, benefit maximization or optimal capital utilization should be a guiding principle; and finally, that the technology chosen should be reliable, and flexible enough to cope with changing needs over time.

Drummond Hislop
July 1991

2 Power from solar energy

Photovoltaics

Photovoltaics (PV) is a technology that converts sunlight directly into electricity. It was first observed in 1839 by the French scientist Becquerel who detected that when light was directed on to one side of a simple battery cell, the current generated could be increased. In the late 1950s, the space programme provided the impetus for the development of crystalline silicon solar cells; the output for terrestrial PV modules matured in 1953 with the introduction of automated PV production plants.

Today, PV systems have an important use in areas remote from a national electricity grid, where they provide power for a wide range of applications including water pumping, lighting, vaccine refrigeration, telecommunications and electrified fencing for livestock. Some tens of thousands of systems are currently in use, yet this number is insignificant compared to the vast potential that exists for PV as an energy source.

A solar PV pump system in Cape Verde

Advantages of PV systems

The provision of an electricity supply to rural areas or remote locations is difficult and expensive; the extension of the mains grid over arduous terrain is seldom economic for small power loads. The problem of economic viability also applies to diesel generator sets, which rely heavily on the availability of fuel supplies and maintenance.

Photovoltaic modules provide an independent, reliable electrical power source at the point of use, making them particularly suited to remote locations. PV systems are technically viable and can be economically feasible for many small-scale applications. Some of their principal advantages are:

○ *No fuel requirements*   In remote areas, diesel or kerosene fuel supplies are erratic and often very expensive. The recurrent costs of operating and maintaining PV systems are small.

○ *Modular design*   A solar array is composed of individual PV modules which can be connected to meet a particular demand.

○ *Reliability of PV modules*   This has been shown to be significantly higher than that of diesel generators or wind generators.

○ *Easy to maintain*   Operation and routine maintenance requirements are simple.

○ *Long life*   With no moving parts and all delicate surfaces protected, modules can be expected to provide power for 15 years or more.

○ *National economic benefits*   Reliance on imported fuels such as coal and oil is reduced.

○ *Environmentally benign*   There is no pollution through the use of a PV system.

The main disadvantage of PV systems is their high capital cost.

The PV process

When light falls on the active surface, the photons in a solar cell become energized, in proportion to the intensity and spectral distribution of the light. When their energy level exceeds a certain point, a potential difference, or open circuit voltage, is established across the cell. This is then capable of driving a current through an external load.

All modern, commercial PV devices use silicon as the base material, mainly as mono-crystalline or multi-crystalline cells, but recently also in amorphous form. A mono-crystalline silicon cell (Figure 1) is made from a thin wafer of a high-purity silicon crystal, doped with a minute quantity of boron. Phosphorus is diffused into the active surface of the wafer. At the front, electrical contact is made by a metallic grid; at the back, contact

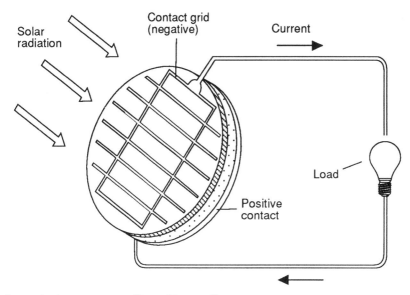

Figure 1 *A mono-crystalline silicon cell*

usually covers the whole surface. An anti-bacterial reflective coating is applied to the front surface.

The process of producing efficient solar cells is costly due to the use of expensive pure silicon and the energy consumed. Research is being carried out to develop new manufacturing technologies.

Modules and arrays

Solar cells are interconnected in series and in parallel to achieve the desired operating voltage and current. They are then protected by encapsulation between glass and a tough resin back. This is all held together by a stainless steel or aluminium frame to form a module (Figure 2). These modules form the basic building blocks of a solar array. Modules may be connected in series or parallel to increase the voltage and current, and thus achieve the required solar array characteristics that will match the load.

Commercially available modules fall into three categories based on the type of solar cell used.

○ *Mono-crystalline cell modules* The highest cell efficiencies of around 15 per cent are obtained with these modules. The cells are cut from a mono-crystalline silicon crystal.

○ *Multi-crystalline cell modules* The cell manufacturing process is lower in cost but cell efficiencies of only around 12 per cent are achieved. A multi-crystalline cell is cut from a cast ingot of multi-crystalline silicon and is generally square in shape.

○ *Amorphous silicon modules*   These are made from thin films of amorphous silicon. Compared with mono-crystalline and multi-crystalline cells, efficiency is much lower – 6 to 9 per cent – but the process uses less material and the potential for cost reduction is greater. Unlike the other cell types, with amorphous silicon there is some degradation of power output with time.

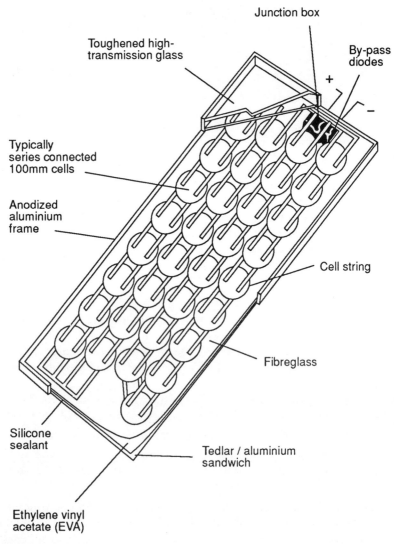

Figure 2 *A module of solar cells in a steel or aluminium frame*

14

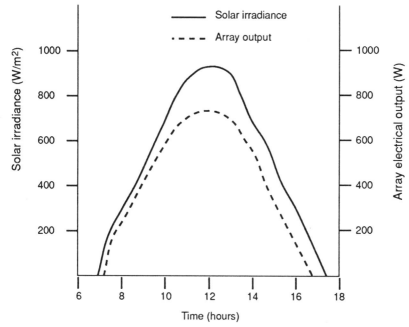

Figure 3 *Power variation daily with changes in solar irradiance and ambient air temperature*

An array can vary from one or two modules with an output of 10 W or less to a vast bank generating several kilowatts or even megawatts. Flat-plate arrays which are held fixed at a tilted angle and face towards the equator are most common. The angle of tilt should be approximately equal to the angle of latitude at the site. A steeper angle increases the output in winter; a shallower angle gives greater output in the summer. It should be at least 10° to allow for rainwater runoff.

Tracking arrays follow the path of the sun during the day and thus theoretically capture more sun. However, the increased complexity and cost of the equipment rarely makes it worthwhile.

Mobile (portable) arrays can be useful with equipment such as lighting systems or small irrigation pumping systems which may be required in different locations.

Performance

The power produced by a PV array depends on the incident solar radiation and the ambient air temperature. As the level of solar irradiance increases, so too will the output power. Conversely, as the ambient air temperature and the solar irradiance increase, the cell temperature will also increase, causing a slight decrease in power (as the cell temperature increases, the efficiency of conversion from sunlight to electricity decreases). Figure 3 illustrates how the power produced may vary over a day with changes in solar irradiance and ambient air temperature.

Since the power output is variable, a module is rated in terms of its output at reference conditions, that is, a standard irradiance level of 1000 W/m² and a cell temperature of 25°C, and is referred to as peak watts (Wp). The average power output over daylight hours will depend on the incident solar radiation and will be much less that the rated output. Table 1 shows the average annual power produced for a 1000 Wp array at various locations around the world (note that the output from a complete system may be less than the figure given because of inefficiencies in the battery and control equipment).

Table 1 Average power produced in daylight hours for a 1000 Wp array

Location	Average power produced (watts)	Average energy produced (kWh/day)
Jedda	490	5.9
Nairobi	450	5.5
Bangkok	420	5.0
Buenos Aires	400	4.7
Lagos	390	4.6
New York	310	3.7
London	230	2.8

Energy output of PV systems

The term 'system' is used to describe the complete set of equipment used in converting solar energy to the final requirement. In most applications, it will be necessary to use a battery so that the output from the whole power supply can be kept constant. Batteries are also used to store energy for days when there is little sunshine. Batteries must be protected with some type of charge control system so that they are neither over-charged nor excessively discharged. For some applications, such as water pumping, batteries are not required because output can vary throughout the day without causing problems.

Because of the daytime variation, it is more useful to talk in terms of energy over the day (kWh) rather than power at a particular time of the day (kW). A rule-of-thumb formula to calculate the approximate daily output of a PV array at a particular location is:

$$E_d = 0.00085 \ (I_d A_r)$$

where:

E_d = average daily electrical energy output (kWh)
I_d = average daily solar irradiation on array (kWh/m²)
A_r = array rated size (Wp)

For example, a solar irradiation level of 5 kWh/m² on a 1 kWp array produces an electrical output of approximately 4.25 kWh.

The rule-of-thumb formula can be rearranged to estimate the size of array needed to provide a required energy output:

$$A_r = 1200E_d/I_d$$

In most locations there are marked variations in solar radiation from month to month. The designer of the system must ensure that it can meet its load in the month when the ratio of energy required to solar irradiation available is highest.

Costs and economics

At present, (1991) PV module prices range from US $5/Wp for orders in the MWp range to US $10/Wp for 1 kWp sizes and up to US $25/Wp for systems less than 100 Wp: small purchases are more expensive per watt than large ones. Price reductions to below US $2 to 3/Wp have been predicted by PV research workers.

The economics of PV are site-specific. They depend on the solar radiation and the cost of competing energy technologies. In sunny areas remote from an electricity grid, where fuel is expensive, PV can be economic for loads up to 20 kWh/day.

Since the cost of a PV system is roughly proportional to the Wp rating, it is always important to have an efficient system for converting the electrical output of the array to its final useful form of energy, for example hydraulic or cooling power. Inefficient systems will increase capital costs.

Applications

Some typical applications of PV are presented below. The sections which then follow describe three of these applications – pumping, refrigeration and lighting – in more detail.

Rural electrification

○ lighting and power supplies for buildings in remote areas such as mosques, farms, schools and mountain refuge huts;

○ power supplies for remote villages;

○ street lighting;

○ individual housing systems;

○ battery charging;

○ mini-grids.

Water pumping and treatment systems

- o pumping for drinking water;
- o pumping for irrigation;
- o dewatering and drainage;
- o ice production;
- o salt water desalination systems;
- o water purification.

Health care systems

- o lighting in rural clinics;
- o UHF transceivers between health centres;
- o vaccine refrigeration;
- o ice-pack freezing for vaccine carriers;
- o sterilizers;
- o blood-storage refrigerators.

Communications

- o radio repeaters;
- o television and radio receivers in remote areas;
- o weather measuring in remote locations;
- o mobile radios;
- o rural telephone kiosks;
- o data acquisition and transmission (for example, river levels and seismographs).

Transport aids

- o lighting for road signs;
- o railway crossings and signals;
- o hazard and warning lights;
- o navigation buoys;
- o fog horns;
- o runway lights;
- o terrain avoidance lights;
- o road markers.

Security systems

- security lighting;
- alarm systems;
- electric fences.

Corrosion protection systems

- cathodic protection for bridges, pipelines and steel structures;
- well-head protection;
- protection for lock gates;
- steel structure protection.

Miscellaneous

- ventilation systems;
- camper and recreational vehicle power;
- calculators;
- pumping and automated feeding systems on fish farms;
- solar water heater circulation pumps;
- path lights;
- yacht/boat power;
- vehicle battery trickle chargers;
- earthquake monitoring systems;
- battery charging;
- fountains;
- emergency power for disaster relief.

Water pumping

The use of solar pumps

Solar pumps have three principal applications: village water supply, live-stock watering and irrigation. The majority of the 6000 or more solar pumping systems installed to date are used for village water supply or livestock watering.

A typical system for village water supply is shown schematically in Figure 4. Domestic water use per capita tends to vary greatly depending on availability. The long-term aim is to provide people with water in sufficient

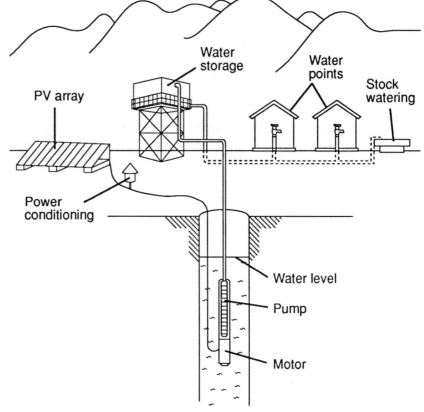

Figure 4 *A typical system for village water supply*

quantities to meet all their requirements for drinking, washing and sanitation. Present short-term goals aim for a per capita provision of 40 1/day; thus a village of 500 people has a requirement of 20 m³/day. Most villages require water for both domestic needs and livestock.

With village water supply there is a constant demand for water throughout the year and a need, therefore, to store water for use during periods of low solar radiation. In environments where rainy seasons occur, the reduced output of the solar pump during these periods can be offset by rainwater harvesting.

A solar irrigation system (Figure 5) needs to take account of the fact that demand for water will vary throughout the year. Peak demand during the irrigation seasons is often more than twice the average demand. This means that solar pumps for irrigation are under-utilized for most of the year. Attention should be paid to the system of water distribution and application to the crops. The system should minimize water losses without imposing significant additional head on the pumping system. It should also be low in cost.

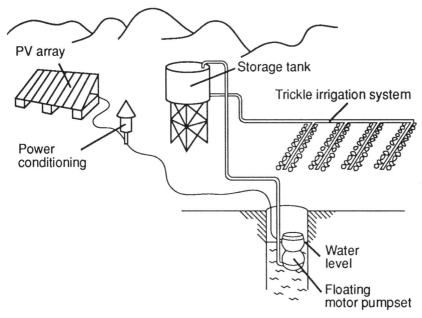

Figure 5 *A solar irrigation system*

This means that flood and sprinkler irrigation systems are not suitable for use with solar pumps; trickle and open-channel systems are better suited because of their higher application efficiency and low head losses.

The technology

Systems can be broadly configured into five types, described below.

Submerged multi-stage centrifugal motor pumpset
This is probably the most common type of solar pump used for village water supply (Figure 6). It is easy to install, often with lay-flat flexible pipework, and the motor pumpset is submerged, away from potential damage. Either alternating current (a.c.) or direct current (d.c.) motors can be incorporated into the pumpset, although an inverter would be needed to convert d.c. electricity into a.c. electricity. If a brushed d.c. motor is used, then the equipment will need to be pulled up from the well every two years or so to replace the brushes. If brushless d.c. motors are incorporated, then electronic commutation will be required. The most commonly employed system consists of an a.c. pump and inverter with a PV array of less than 1500 Wp.

Submerged pump with surface mounted motor
This configuration was widely installed with turbine pumps in Sahelian West Africa during the 1970s. It gives easy access to the motor for brush

changing and other maintenance. The low efficiency from power losses in the shaft bearings and the high cost of installation have been disadvantages, and the system is largely being replaced by the submersible motor and pumpset.

Reciprocating positive displacement pump (Figure 7)
The reciprocating positive displacement pump – often known as the jack or nodding donkey – is very suitable for high-head, low-flow applications. The output is proportional to the speed of the pump. At high heads the frictional forces are low compared with the hydrostatic forces, often making positive displacement pumps more efficient than centrifugal pumps in similar situations. Reciprocating positive displacement pumps create a cyclic load on the motor which, for efficient operation, needs to be balanced. Hence the above-ground components of the solar pump are often heavy and robust, and power controllers for impedance matching are often used.

Floating motor pumpsets (Figure 8)
The versatility of the floating unit set makes it ideal for irrigation pumping for canals and open wells. The pumpset is easily portable and there is a negligible chance of the pump running dry. Most of these types use a single-stage submersed centrifugal pump. The most common use a brushless – electronically commutated – d.c. motor. Often, the solar array support incorporates a handle or wheelbarrow-type trolley to enable transportation.

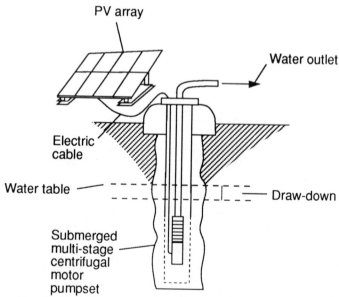

Figure 6 *Submerged multi-stage centrifugal motor pump set*

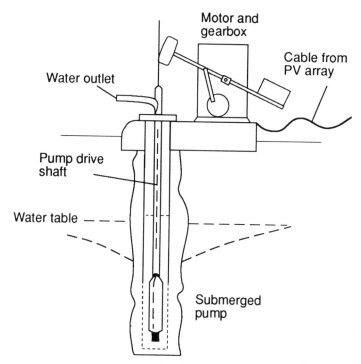

Figure 7 *Reciprocating positive displacement pump, or jack, or nodding donkey*

Surface suction pumpsets
This type of pumpset is not recommended unless an operator can always be in attendance. Although the use of primary chambers and non-return valves can prevent loss of prime, in practice self-start and priming problems are experienced. It is impractical to use suction heads of more than 8 m.

Performance

Solar pumps are available which can pump in the range of up to 200 m head and with outputs of up to 250 m³/day. Solar pumping technology continues to improve. In the early 1980s, the typical solar energy to hydraulic (pumped water) energy efficiency was around 2 per cent, with the PV array achieving 6 to 8 per cent efficiency, while the motor and pumpset was typically 25 per cent efficient. In 1991, an efficient solar pump has an average daily solar energy to hydraulic efficiency of more than 4 per cent. PV modules of the mono-crystalline type now have efficiencies in excess of 12 per cent, and more efficient motors and pumpsets are available. A good subsystem (that is the motor, pump and any power conditioning) should have an average daily energy throughput efficiency of 30 to 40 per cent.

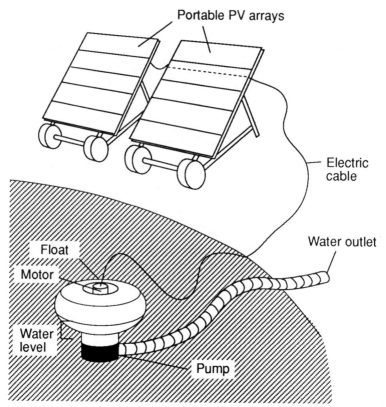

Figure 8 *Floating motor pumpset*

Calculating system size

The size of a solar pump will depend on the volume of water required, the total head and the solar irradiation. For livestock and village water systems, the amount of water can be assessed from the population to be served.

Irrigation requirements depend upon crop water needs, effective ground-water contributions and the efficiency of the distribution and field application system. These requirements can be determined by consultation with local experts and agronomists or by reference to the FAO document *Crop-water requirements*.

Several water source parameters need to be taken into account, and measured where possible: the depth of the water source below ground level, the height of the storage tank or water outlet point above ground level and seasonal variations in water level. The draw-down or drop in water level after pumping has commenced also needs to be considered for well and borehole supplies. This will depend on the ratio between the pumping rate and the rate of refill of the water source.

The pattern of water use should also be considered in relation to system design and storage requirements. Water supply systems should include sufficient covered water storage to provide for daily water requirements and short periods of cloudy weather. Generally, two to five days' water demand is stored.

The required array size can then be calculated using the following formulae:

$$E_h = \rho_w g H V / (3.6 \times 10^6)$$

where:

E_h = hydraulic energy required (kWh/day)
ρ_w = density of water (1000 kg/m³)
g = gravitational acceleration (9.81 m/s²)
H = total hydraulic head (m)
V = volume of water required (m³/day)

which reduces to $E_h = 0.002725HV$ (kWh/day).
The solar array size required is:

$$A_r = E_h/(eFI_d)$$

where:

I_d = average daily solar irradiation (kWh/m²)
F = array mismatch factor (0.85 on average)
e = daily subsystem efficiency (typically 0.25 to 0.40)

Costs and economics

A PV pumping system to pump 25 m³/day through 20 m head requires a solar array of approximately 800 Wp in the Sahelian regions. Such a pump would cost approximately US $12,000 free on board (FOB). Further examples are given in Table 2.

Table 2 Costs of PV pumping systems

Motor pump/ configuration	Output (m³/day) @ kWhm²/day insolation	Head (m)	Solar array (Wp)	System price (US$ FOB)
Submerged borehole	40	20	1200	16 000–18 000
motor pump	25	20	800	10 000–12 000
Surface motor/ submerged pump	60	7	840	9000–12 000
Reciprocating positive displacement pump	6	100	1200	16 000–19 000
Floating motor/	100	3	530	8000
pumpset	10	3	85	3000
Surface suction pump	40	4	350	6000

A range of prices is to be expected, since the total system comprises the cost of modules, pump, motor, pipework, wiring, control system, array support structure and packaging. Systems with larger array sizes generally have a lower cost per peak watt. The cost of the motor pumpset varies according to application and duties: a low-lift suction pump may cost less than US $800 whereas a submersible borehole pumpset costs US$1500 or more.

In general, PV pumps are economic compared with diesel pumps up to approximately 3 kWp for village water supply and around 1 kWp for irrigation.

Refrigeration of vaccines

The need

Extensive immunization programmes are in progress throughout the developing world in the fight against the common communicable diseases. To be effective, these programmes must provide immunization services to rural areas. All vaccines have to be kept within a limited temperature range throughout transportation and storage. The provision of refrigeration for this, known as the vaccine 'cold chain', is a major logistical undertaking in areas where electricity supplies are non-existent or erratic.

Solar radiation tends to be high in climates that have the greatest need for cooling, and much effort has been directed to develop solar-powered refrigerators. Although some solar absorption refrigerators have been produced, so far only solar electric (PV) refrigerators have proved reliable.

Solar PV power for refrigerators has great potential with its low running costs, reliability and long working life. The performance of refrigerators fuelled by kerosene and bottled gas is often inadequate and diesel powered systems frequently suffer fuel supply problems. Solar power is therefore of great importance to health care, and over the past five years, at least 3000 PV medical refrigerators have been installed.

Relative merits of PV refrigerators

Compared to refrigerators fuelled by kerosene or bottled gas, PV systems have many advantages.

Improved vaccine storage facilities as a result of:

o   elimination of fuel supply problems;

o   elimination of fuel quality problems;

o   greater refrigerator reliability;

o   better refrigerator performance and temperature control.

26

Reduced running costs as a result of:

o elimination of kerosene fuel costs;

o reduced vaccine losses;

o lower refrigerator maintenance costs;

o reduced need for back-up refrigerators where there are fuel supply or repair problems.

Cold chain management benefits due to:

o longer equipment life (PV array – 15 years; battery – 5 years and refrigerator – 10 years);

o reduced logistical problems arising from non-availability of working refrigerators;

o reduced logistical problems arising from vaccine losses.

These operational advantages indicate that solar refrigerators can provide a sustainable vaccine cold chain. It should be noted, however, that as each system is site-specific, more time is necessary for planning and implementing a project using solar refrigerators. User training demands are also higher since a new technology is being introduced.

The technology

The refrigerator

Photovoltaic refrigerators operate on the same principle as normal compression refrigerators, but incorporate low voltage – 12 or 24 V (volts) – d.c. compressors and motors rather than mains voltage a.c. types. A PV refrigerator has higher levels of insulation around the storage compartments to maximize energy efficiency, a battery bank for electricity storage, a battery charge regulator and a controller which converts the power from the battery to a form required by the compressor motor.

A typical refrigerator layout is shown in Figure 9. Most refrigerators include a freezer compartment for ice-pack freezing. Other systems have separate units to provide solely for refrigeration or freezing. Sizes available range between 10 and 200 litres of vaccine storage capacity, with ice production rates of up to 5 kg/24 h.

Batteries

The battery most commonly used is the lead-acid type, and long-life, deep-cycle batteries are preferable. A capacity to run the refrigerator for five days without sun is recommended.

Charge regulator

The charge regulator maintains the power supply within the current and voltage range tolerated by the refrigerator and prevents over-charging of

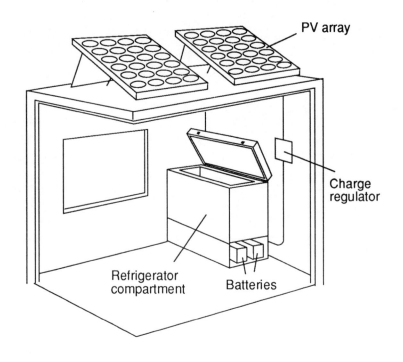

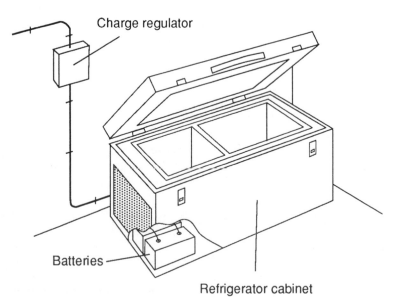

Figure 9 *Typical solar refrigerator*

the battery. Some models include an audible alarm or warning light to signal that battery voltage has become low. Lightning surge protection is an important provision for tropical areas.

Array and support structure
The solar array can be mounted on a roof or at ground level. The typical array size is 150 to 200 Wp.

Performance

The energy consumption of a PV vaccine refrigerator is typically 300 to 500 Wh/24 h for a 100 litre refrigerator without ice-pack freezing and at +32°C ambient temperature. At +43°C ambient temperature and freezing 2 kg of ice-packs per 24 h, the energy consumption of the same refrigerator would rise to about 600 to 1200 Wh/24 h. It is very important not to overload a solar refrigerator as this increases energy consumption considerably.

A good vaccine refrigerator should be able to maintain correct internal temperatures for at least ten hours in the event of disconnection from the battery and solar array.

Costs

A true comparison of solar refrigerators and comparable kerosene and bottled gas fuelled refrigerators can only be made through a life-cycle cost analysis.

A refrigerator is likely to cost around US $3000 to $4000 and will cost more to install than a kerosene unit. A kerosene refrigerator will cost only US $600 to $800 but will use 0.5 to 1 litre of fuel per day, require frequent maintenance and have a shorter life. In general, life-cycle costs are approximately the same for solar and kerosene refrigerators, but because of their greater reliability and subsequent savings in wasted vaccine, solar refrigerators are the preferred option.

Lighting

The need

Quality lighting is a basic need for human development. Generally, most lighting in the rural areas of developing countries is provided by candles or kerosene lamps, while torches or flashlights powered by expensive, throwaway dry cells are used as a portable source of light for intermittent use. The light provided is of poor quality and can be expensive.

Light intensity is measured in lumens. A reasonable level of illumination for reading may require at least 200 lumens. A candle provides an output of 1 lumen, while a wick oil lamp can offer 10 lumens. In contrast a 10 Wp PV light can have an output of 400 lumens. Thus, PV lighting systems can be a cheap way to provide adequate rural lighting.

The technology

A PV lighting system comprises a module, a lamp (and inverter for some lamps), a battery and a controller. There are several commercial systems available; some have all components integrated into one unit while others use a separate module which can be mounted on a roof or pole. Experience in the Dominican Republic and Kenya has shown that systems can be assembled locally at much lower costs.

Lamps and inverters

The principal properties that need to be considered for PV lighting systems are the efficacy, measured as the light output in lumens per watt of electrical power supplied, the voltage (d.c. or a.c.), the lifetime of the lamp, the cost and the colour of the light. Three main types of lamp could be used: incandescent tungsten, incandescent halogen or fluorescent. Table 3 summarizes their principal characteristics.

vb**Table 3   Lights for use with PV systems**

Type of light	Power (W)	Intensity (lumens)	Efficacy (lumens/W)	Rated life (hours)
Tungsten	40	400	10	1000
Tungsten	100	1300	13	1000
Halogen	20	350	17	2000
Fluorescent	15	600	40	7500

vb   Incandescent tungsten lamps produce yellowish or white light by heating a tungsten filament to 4000°C or 6000°C respectively. The incandescent principle of converting electricity to light is relatively inefficient since more heat than light is produced.

Tungsten lamps can operate from low voltage d.c. and are therefore better matched to PV modules than fluorescent lamps which require high voltage a.c. electricity. However, their low efficiency is a serious disadvantage. Their lifetime depends on the operating voltage: the lower the voltage the longer the life.

Halogen lamps also produce light from the incandescent principle but have greater efficacy and a longer lifetime. Some manufacturers produce lamps with built-in reflectors, and efficacies of up to 30 lumens/W can be achieved.

Fluorescent lamps are the usual choice for PV lighting systems because of their higher efficacy. They produce a 'whiter' light than incandescent lamps. Their main disadvantage is that they operate on high voltage a.c. and therefore need an inverter which adds to the cost and reduces the overall efficiency by between 65 and 90 per cent, depending on the inverter used. Despite these losses, the overall efficacy is better than that of tungsten and halogen lamps. Some small fluorescent lights include a built-in inverter, and often run at a higher frequency than the mains, which improves the light's efficiency still further. Problems have been experienced with fluorescent lamps 'blackening' when operated at low d.c. voltages: this may be due to the properties of the inverter.

Batteries
Electric light is normally needed on demand, and the only way of ensuring this requirement is to provide electrical storage in the form of a battery. The two main battery options available are lead-acid and nickel-cadmium batteries: the former is similar to the batteries used in cars. Nickel-cadmium batteries are less generally available (except as dry cell substitutes) and cost more, but they can be more robust and tolerant of abuse than lead-acid batteries. However, they self-discharge quite quickly if not used.

For most lighting purposes, lead-acid batteries are probably the easiest and cheapest cell option. They are available as deep-discharge batteries which have a longer life than car batteries and, if looked after, tend to be better for general electrical storage. Most lead-acid and nickel-cadmium batteries require regular checking of their electrolyte level and topping up with distilled or de-ionized water (not with acid). Rainwater can be used for this purpose, providing it has not been contaminated in any way. Low-maintenance and maintenance-free lead-acid batteries are also available now, at a slightly increased cost.

An important point to note with lead-acid batteries is that their life is considerably shortened if they are over-discharged, that is, electrically discharged beyond the recommended level for optimum life. Ideally, they should only be discharged to about 50 per cent of their full rating; that is, a 60 ampere-hour (Ah) battery should only be discharged to 30 Ah before recharging.

Controller and cabling
The controller is connected between the PV module and the battery to protect the battery against over-charging and excess discharge. It can also optimize the power available from the PV module, control the use of the light, and provide warning indicators. Controllers can be expensive, leading to a high percentage increase in cost for small power systems. Some solar electric systems do not include controllers: this will inevitably affect the life of the battery. Moreover, the use of cheap batteries may not be cost effective.

Cable runs should be kept as short as possible with low voltage supplies, or else very heavy cable must be used, as otherwise significant losses will occur in the cables. Copper cable of 1 mm is adequate for runs up to 50 m.

System sizing

A rough estimate of the size of a lighting system can be made by estimating the daily electrical load. This is simply the rated power of the lamp multiplied by the number of operating hours per day. For example, a 10 W fluorescent light running for 4 h/night will require 40 Wh of electricity each

24 hours. Take into account the losses in the inverter, cables and the battery – which can amount to 30 to 50 per cent – and this figure will increase to about 65 Wh/24 h.

The battery must be sized to avoid a discharge of more than 50 per cent. Using the same example, a battery with a total discharge capacity of 130 Wh would be required to provide a nominal storage capacity of 24 h.

The PV module size can be calculated using the formula given above on page 25. For example, in a location with 5 kWh/m²/day the module would have to be $(0.065/(5 \times 0.00085) = 15$ Wp.

Costs

Commercial packaged units range from US $100 for portable lanterns to US $2000 for systems with two to three lights. With a little expertise, systems can be assembled from components at the individual component prices given below.

- ○ Modules: US $10–20/Wp for modules less than 30 Wp

- ○ Lamps: US $20

- ○ Batteries: US $100/kWh

For example, the cost of a system for the example cited above would be in the order of US $200 to $300. This may seem a great deal to pay for a single light, but the running costs will be negligible and good quality light will be reliably available. A pressure lantern, which is much less satisfactory, might only cost about US $15 to $30, but it would consume in the region of 5 litres of kerosene per week on the same duty cycle, raising the costs to between US $75 and $150 per year.

3   Heat from solar energy

Distillation

There is an urgent need for clean, pure drinking water in many developing countries. Water sources are often brackish (salty) or contain harmful bacteria, preventing their use as drinking water. In addition, there are many coastal locations where sea water is abundant but potable water is not available. Pure water is also useful for batteries and in hospitals or schools.

Distillation is one of many processes which can be used for water purification. In this process water is evaporated (thus separating water vapour from dissolved matter) and condensed as pure water. Distillation requires an energy input as heat, and solar radiation is a potential source of this energy.

Solar water distillation is a technology with a very long history; some installations were built over 2000 years ago, although their function was to produce salt rather than drinking water! Documented use of solar stills began in the sixteenth century. An early large-scale solar still was built in 1872 to supply a mining community in Chile with drinking water. Mass production occurred for the first time during the Second World War when 200000 inflatable plastic stills were made to be kept in life rafts for the US Navy.

There are a number of other approaches to water purification and desalination, such as photovoltaic-powered reverse-osmosis, for which small-scale commercially available equipment is available. In addition, if treatment of polluted water is required rather than desalination, slow sand filtration is a good option: details of publications on slow sand filtration can be found in Annexe I on page 98.

The sections which follow provide basic information on solar distillation, and direct the reader to more detailed sources.

Energy requirements

The energy required to evaporate water is latent heat from the vaporization of water. This has a value of 2260 kilojoules per kilogram (kJ/kg). This means that a heat input of 2260 kJ is required to produce 1 litre (that is 1 kg, since the density of water is 1 kg/l) of pure water by distilling brackish water. This does not allow for the efficiency of the heating method, which will be less than 100 per cent, or for any recovery of latent heat.

It should be noted that although 2260 kJ/kg is required to evaporate water, only 0.2 kJ/kg is needed to pump 1 kg of water through 20 m head. Distillation is therefore normally considered only where there is no local source of fresh water that can be easily pumped or lifted.

Operation and design objectives

Figure 10 shows a single-basin still. The main features of operation are the same for all solar stills. The incident solar radiation is transmitted through the glass cover and is absorbed as heat by a black surface in contact with the water to be distilled. The water is thus heated and gives off water vapour. The vapour condenses on the glass cover, which is at a lower temperature because it is in contact with the ambient air, and runs down into a gutter which leads to a storage tank.

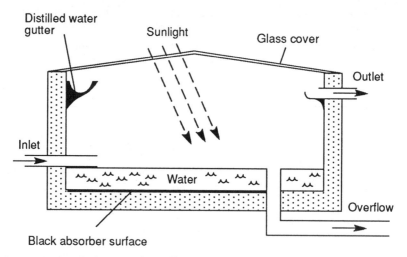

Figure 10 *Single-basin solar still*

For greatest efficiency the solar still should achieve three objectives: a high feed (undistilled) water temperature; a large temperature difference between feed water and condensing surface and a low vapour leakage.

A high feed water temperature can be achieved if:

○ a high proportion of incoming radiation is absorbed by the feed water as heat: hence low absorption glazing and a good radiation-absorbing surface are required;

○ heat losses from the floor and walls are kept low;

○ the water is shallow so that it can be heated more quickly and to a higher temperature.

A large temperature difference can be achieved if:

- o the condensing surface absorbs little or none of the incoming radiation;

- o condensing water dissipates heat which must be removed rapidly from the surface by, for example, a second flow of water or air, or condensing at night.

A low vapour leakage can be achieved by:

- o effective sealing of the glass cover on the solar still.

Design types and their performance

Single-basin still
Single-basin stills have been much studied and their behaviour is well understood. Efficiencies of 25 per cent are typical. Daily output as a function of solar irradiation is greatest in the early evening when the feed water is still hot but outside temperatures are falling.

Material selection is very important. The cover can be either glass or plastic. Glass is considered to be best for long-term applications, whereas a plastic (such as polyethylene) can be used in the short term.

Sand concrete or waterproofed concrete are considered to be the best materials to use for the basin of a long-life still if it is to be manufactured on-site, but for factory-manufactured stills, prefabricated ferroconcrete is more suitable.

Multiple-effect basin stills
Multiple-effect basin stills have two or more compartments. The condensing surface of the lower compartment is the floor of the upper compartment. The heat given off by the condensing vapour provides energy to vaporize the feed water above. At 35 per cent or more, efficiency is greater than that of a single-basin still, but costs and complexity are higher, too.

Wick stills
In a wick still, the feed water flows slowly through a porous, radiation-absorbing pad (the wick). Two advantages are claimed over basin stills. Firstly, the wick can be tilted so that the feed water presents a better angle to the sun (reducing reflection and presenting a large effective area). Secondly, less feed water is in the still at any time, so the water is heated more quickly and to a higher temperature. Simple wick stills are more efficient than basin stills and there are claims that some designs cost less than basin stills of the same output.

Hybrid designs
There are a number of ways in which solar stills can be usefully combined with another function of technology. Some examples are given below.

o *Rainwater collection*   By adding an external gutter, the still cover can also be used for rainwater collection to supplement the solar still output.

o *Greenhouse solar still*   The roof of a greenhouse can be used as the cover of a still.

o *Supplementary heating*   Waste heat from an engine or the condenser of a refrigerator can be used as an additional energy input.

Output of a solar still

An approximate method of estimating the output of a solar still is given by the formula below:

$$Q = 1.6 \, (eAI_d)$$

where:

Q = daily output of distilled water (litres/day)
e = overall system efficiency
I_d = average daily solar radiation (kWh/day)
A = aperture area of the still (ie, plan area, m^2)

In a tropical country the average daily global solar irradiation is typically 18.0 MJ/m^2 (5 kWh/m^2). A single basin still operates at an overall efficiency of about 30 per cent: hence the daily output per square metre of area is calculated below:

$$\text{Daily output (Q)} = 1.6 \times 0.3 \times 5 = 2.4 \, (l/m^2/day)$$

The yearly output of a solar still may therefore be referred to as approximately one cubic metre per square metre (1m^3/m^2).

Performance and costs

Despite a proliferation of novel designs, the single-basin still remains the only design proven in the field. At least 40 single-basin stills with areas greater than 100 m^2 (and up to 9000 m^2) were built between 1957 and 1980; 27 had glass covers while 9 used plastic. Of the glass-covered stills, 24 are still operating in their original form, but only one plastic-covered unit is still in use in 1991. Hundreds of smaller units are operating, notably in Africa.

The cost of a solar still is normally US$84 to $110/m^2. The price of land will normally be a small proportion of this in rural areas, but may be prohibitive in towns and cities. The life of a glass still is usually taken as 20 to 30 years, but operating costs can be high, especially to replace broken glass.

The charges for pure water will depend on:

o the cost of making the still;

o the cost of the land;

o the life of the still;

o operating costs;

o cost of the feed water;

o the discount rate;

o the amount of water produced.

When is a solar still suitable?

Human beings need one or two litres of water a day to live. The minimum requirement for 'normal' life in developing countries – which includes cooking, cleaning and washing clothes – is 20 l/day (in the industrialized world this may rise to 200 to 400 l/day): but some functions can be performed with salty water. A typical requirement for distilled water is 5 l/day per person; therefore 2 m^2 of still is needed for each person served.

Solar stills should normally only be considered for the removal of dissolved salts from water. If there is a choice between brackish ground water or polluted surface water, it will usually be cheaper to use a slow sand filter or other treatment device. If there is no fresh water then the main alternatives are desalination, transporting water in from other locations and rainwater collection.

For outputs of 1 m^3/day or more, reverse-osmosis or electrodialysis should be considered as an alternative to solar stills. Much will depend on the availability and price of electrical power.

For outputs of 200 m^3/day or more, vapour compression or flash evaporation will normally be the least expensive alternative. Part of the energy requirement of flash evaporation can be met by solar water heaters.

In many parts of the world, fresh water is transported from another region of location by boat, train or truck. Costs are much the same as they are for water produced by solar stills. A pipeline may be less expensive for very large quantities.

Rainwater collection is an even simpler technique than solar distillation in areas where rain is not scarce, but requires a greater area and usually a larger storage tank. If ready-made collection surfaces exist (such as house roofs) these may provide a less expensive source for obtaining clean water.

The initial capital cost of solar stills is roughly proportional to capacity, whereas other methods have significant economies of scale. For the individual household, therefore, the solar still is an economic method of desalination.

Water heating

Hot water is required for many purposes, and the sun can be used effectively, efficiently and economically to provide this heat. The warming effect of solar radiation is obvious and it is well known that a container of cold water left exposed to the sun will be raised in temperature. Solar water heating systems are designed to make convenient use of this occurrence.

Solar water heaters generally employ a solar collector and a storage tank. The solar water heating collector is by far the most widespread solar energy conversion device and there are several millions in use around the world. There are many simple designs of collector and water heating system, and construction and manufacture is easily achievable in most developing countries.

Energy for heating water

The energy required to raise the temperature of a substance is a physical property known as the 'specific heat' of that substance. The specific heat of water is 4.2 J/g/°C, that is 4.2 joules of energy are required to raise the temperature of one gram of water by one degree centigrade. Using larger and more familiar units:

Energy required (kJ) = 4.2 × volume (l) × temperature rise (°C).

Thus, in order to consider energy sources for water heating, the parameters which must be known are the volume of water required in a given time period (hour or day), the temperature of the 'cold' water, and the temperature required. Hot water may be used for a variety of purposes and quantities vary widely. In industrialized countries, an average of 50 l/day person is normal for domestic use while in developing countries the more wealthy inhabitants may use this amount or more, and the poor may not use hot water at all.

For the comparisons which follow, a daily requirement for 100 litres of water at 60°C with an ambient water temperature of 20°C is assumed. Thus the energy requirement is:

$$4.2 \times 100 \times (60 - 20) = 16,800 \text{ kJ}$$
$$= 16.8 \text{ MJ}.$$

It is more convenient for the examples which follow to measure energy in kWh. To convert Megajoules (MJ) into kWh divide by 3.6 (1 kWh = 3.6 MJ), thus 16.8 MJ = 4.7 kWh. This is the amount of energy which must be put into the water. With many water-heating systems the process is not 100 per cent efficient as not all the energy used goes into heating the water, causing heat losses. Some examples are given below.

Electric resistance heating is almost 100 per cent efficient. Hence to heat the water in the above example – 100 litres through a temperature rise of 40°C – would require 4.7 kWh of electricity, the equivalent of running a 1 kW-rated electric immersion heater for nearly five hours. Although electricity is efficient at heating water, it is expensive and not available everywhere.

Water is usually heated by burning fuel. An oil (kerosene)- or gas-fuelled water heater achieves an efficiency of around 50 per cent, while heating water on an open fire has an efficiency of only about 10 per cent. In the latter case, to heat the 100 litres of water to 40°C would require fire-wood with a calorific value of nearly 100 kWh. This is equivalent to about 10 kg of low- (15 per cent) moisture wood.

By comparison, a simple solar water heater might have an efficiency of around 30 per cent. On a very sunny day the solar energy received could reach 6 kWh/m^2. Thus to heat 100 litres of water to 40°C would require a solar collector with an area of $4.7/(6 \times 0.3) = 2.6$ m^2.

The example below is intended to give a rough estimate of the collector area required. However, the energy available from the sun and the performance characteristics of solar collectors vary in a complex way and generalizations should be used with caution.

$$\text{Collector area required} = \frac{\text{energy demand}}{\text{solar energy per m}^2 \times \text{collector efficiency}}$$

The availability of solar energy

The power density of solar energy reaches a maximum of about 1000 W/m^2 at sea level. This is made up of two components: the radiation in the direct beams from the sun and diffuse radiation from the sky (radiation that has been scattered by the atmosphere). On a clear day, diffuse energy may amount to 15 to 20 per cent of global irradiance whereas on a cloudy day it will be 100 per cent.

Global irradiance varies throughout the course of the day because the path length of solar radiation through the atmosphere changes. For the same reason, there are variations with season and latitude: the total solar energy received in a day (known as insolation or solar irradiation) can vary from 0.5 kWh/m^2 in the UK winter to 5 kWh/m^2 in the UK summer and 7 kWh/m^2 in desert regions of the world. Many tropical regions do not have large seasonal variations and receive an average 6 kWh/m^2/day throughout the year.

This variability is an important aspect of solar energy because it influences system design and solar energy economics. The size of a solar collector required for a particular application is dependent on the location.

The technology

When radiant energy strikes the surface of an object, part of it is reflected (depending upon the angle of incidence and the nature of the surface), some is absorbed and a proportion may be transmitted through the object. With a few important exceptions, such as photovoltaic cells, the energy of the absorbed radiation is degraded rapidly to heat.

The temperature attained is determined by a balance between the input of absorbed energy and the heat loss to the environment. The heat loss increases with the temperature and limits the ultimate temperature attained by a collector system. It also reduces the proportion of useful heat extractable from the system. Maximum temperatures and maximum useful power outputs are therefore obtained when a highly absorbent, well-insulated body is exposed to a high intensity of solar radiation. A wide range of systems, designed to meet a variety of needs and situations, have been developed and many are available commercially.

The best known solar heating device is the flat-plate collector, which is widely used for water heating in many parts of the world. The flat-plate collector absorbs as much as possible of the incident solar energy that falls upon it. Since the collector is normally fixed in position, the plate is close to perpendicular to the beam of sunlight (and therefore maximum absorption) for only part of the time, and the level of energy received therefore varies more strongly with time and season than does the actual intensity of the solar radiation. Because of the large areas over which heat can be lost, the retention of heat, and hence the collection efficiency, falls off rapidly with increases in collection temperature. However, since the temperature required of domestic water is normally at only about 50°C, this is not usually a problem.

Design and performance

A simple flat-plate collector is shown in Figure 11. This consists of:

- ○ an absorber which is painted black and from which heat is removed by a heat transfer fluid;

- ○ a cover which is transparent to solar radiation;

- ○ insulation at the back and sides of the absorber;

- ○ a casing to protect the absorber and its insulation.

The absorber may be made from one of a wide range of materials, including copper, stainless steel, galvanized steel, aluminium and plastic. When choosing the material for an absorber it is important to ensure that it is compatible with both the heat transfer fluid and the other components in the system, from the point of view of corrosion. The absorber must also be able to withstand the highest temperature that might be reached on a sunny day when no fluid is flowing in the collector (known as the stagnation temperature). The fluid passageways of the absorber may consist of tubes bonded on to an absorbing plate, or may form an integral part of the absorber.

Experience has shown that simple mechanical clamping of tubes on to an absorber plate is likely to result in poor efficiency. A good thermal bond, such as a braze, weld or high-temperature solder, is required for the tube and plate designs in order to ensure good heat transfer from the absorber surface into the fluid.

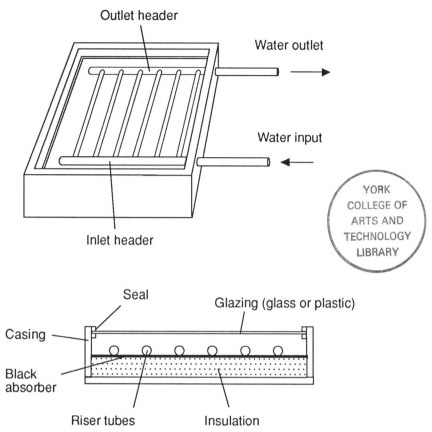

Figure 11 *Simple flat-plate collector*

Matt black paints are commonly used for absorber surfaces because they are relatively cheap, simple to apply and may be easily repaired. Paints, however, have the disadvantage that they are usually strong emitters of thermal radiation (infra-red) and, at high temperatures, this results in significant heat losses from the front of the collector.

Heat losses from the collector can be substantially reduced by the use of absorber coatings known as 'selective surfaces'. These surfaces may be applied by electroplating or by dipping a metal absorber into the appropriate chemicals to produce a thin semiconducting film over the surface. The thin film will be transparent to solar radiation, but at the same time will appear opaque to thermal radiation. However, these surfaces cannot be produced or applied easily.

Flat-plate collectors usually have a transparent cover made of glass or plastic. The cover is required to reduce heat losses from the front of the collector and to protect the absorber and the insulation from the weather. Most

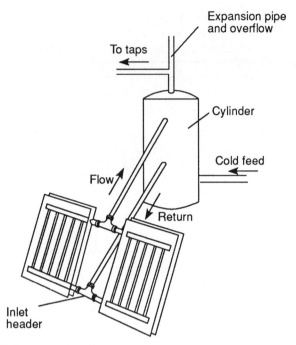

Figure 12 *Solar water heating system*

covers behave like a greenhouse. They permit solar radiation to pass into the collector, but they absorb the thermal radiation emitted by the hot absorber.

A solar water heating system consists essentially of a flat-plate collector and a water storage tank; the simplest arrangement is illustrated in Figure 12. The tank is placed at a higher level than the collector, so that the heated water will run from the collector to the tank and induce natural circulation by convection (thermosyphon). These systems can be very reliable provided the diameter of the pipework is adequate and there are no sharp bends. This is the most common design of solar water heater for use in developing countries.

At night it is possible for the collector to lose heat by radiation and, as the circulation will be in the opposite direction, so the water will cool. This can be overcome by the use of a suitable non-return valve. However when solar collectors are used under clear night conditions there is a danger that they will actually freeze even when the ambient temperature is above freezing point. This problem only occurs in certain desert regions during the cold season or at high altitudes in the tropics and subtropics. Under such conditions, it may be necessary to have a primary circuit through the collector filled with antifreeze, and a separate indirect hot water cylinder where the water from the collector passes through a copper coil to heat the main water supply.

It is also possible to pump the water between the collector and the tank.

This allows the two components to be situated further apart, and negates the need for the tank to be at a higher level than the collector. However, these systems are much more complex, and electricity is required to power the circulating pump.

Costs

Flat-plate solar collectors typically cost US$250/m^2; a professionally installed system costs around US$3500 or more installed. In the UK the economies are marginal because savings on fuel will only be about US$170 a year. In sunnier locations, however, payback periods of just a few years are possible. In addition, the use of water heating is beneficial to the environment as it displaces the burning of other fuels.

Drying

A wide range of products have been dried by the sun and wind in the open air for thousands of years. In the case of foodstuffs, the purpose of drying is to preserve them for later use; with industries such as timber, tobacco and tea it is an integral part of the production process. In industrialized regions and sectors, open-air drying has now been largely replaced by mechanized driers with boilers to heat incoming air, and fans to force it through at a high rate. Mechanized drying is faster than open-air drying, uses much less land, and usually gives a better-quality product. However, the equipment is expensive and its operation requires substantial quantities of fuel or electricity.

In this chapter solar drying refers to methods of using the sun's energy for drying, but excludes open-air 'sun drying'. The justification for solar driers is that they may be more effective than sun drying, but have lower operating costs than mechanized driers.

Design and technology

A well-known design of solar drier is shown in Figure 13. It was developed with the particular requirements of rice in mind, but the principles hold for

Table 4   Moisture absorption capacity of air

Initial relative humidity	Moisture absorption capability (grammes of water/m^3 of air)		
	Not heated	Heated to:	
(%)		40°C	60°C
40	4.33	9.2	16.3
60	1.4	8.2	15.6
80	0	7.1	14.6

Note: Air enters at 20°C, and leaves at 80 per cent relative humidity.

43

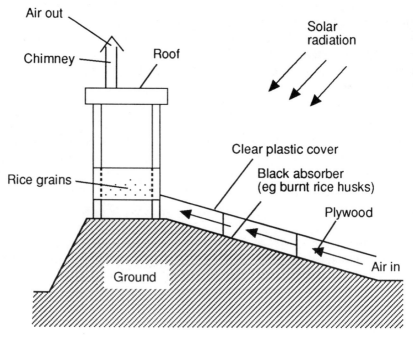

Figure 13 *Solar drier*

other products and design types since the basic need is the same: the removal of water.

Air is drawn through the drier by natural convection. It is heated as it passes through the collector, then partially cooled as it picks up moisture from the rice. The rice is heated both by the air and directly by the sun.

The moisture absorption capability of air is affected by its initial humidity and by the temperature to which it is subsequently heated: this is demonstrated in Table 4.

The objective of most drying processes is to reduce the moisture content of the product to a specified value. Moisture content is expressed as the weight of water as a proportion of the total weight. The moisture content of rice has typically to be reduced from 24 per cent to 14 per cent. So, in order to dry 1 tonne of rice, 100 kg of water must be removed. If the heated air has a 'spare capacity' of 8 g then $100/0.008 = 12\,500$ m³ of air are required to dry 1 tonne of rice.

Some 250 MJ (70 kWh) of energy is required to vaporize the water. Although this quantity is fixed, there is no fixed requirement for the solar heat input to the drier. This is because the incoming ambient air can give up some of its internal energy to vaporize the water, becoming colder in the process. Indeed, if the ambient air is dry enough, then no heat input is required.

Nevertheless, extra heat *is* useful, for two reasons. Firstly if the air is warmer, then less of it is needed. Secondly, the temperature in the rice grains themselves may be an important factor, especially in the later stages of drying when moisture has to be 'drawn' from the centre of the grains to their surfaces. This temperature will itself depend mainly on the air temperature, but also on the amount of solar radiation received directly by the rice.

In a natural convection system the flow of air is caused by the fact that the warm air inside the drier is lighter than the cooler air outside. This difference in density creates a small pressure difference across the bed of grain which forces the air through it. Looking at Figure 13, this effect increases with the greater the height of the bed above the inlet (h_1) and the outlet above the bed (h_2). The effect of an increased h_2 is less than that of an increased h_1 because the air is cooled as it passes through the bed.

Table 5   Air density changes at different temperatures in solar driers

Initial relative humidity	Density of the air (kg/m³) (drop in density in brackets)							
	Not heated:			Heated to:				
(%)				30%		40%		60%
40	Ambient	1.19		1.19		1.19		1.19
	Below bed	1.19	(0.00)	1.15 (0.04)	1.12 (0.07)		1.05 (0.14)	
	Above bed	1.21	(−0.02)	1.19 (0.00)	1.17 (0.02)		1.14 (0.05)	
60	Ambient	1.19		1.19		1.19		1.19
	Below bed	1.19	(0.00)	1.15 (0.04)	1.11 (0.08)		1.05 (0.14)	
	Above bed	1.20	(−0.01)	1.18 (0.01)	1.16 (0.03)		1.13 (0.06)	
80	Ambient	1.18		1.18		1.18		1.18
	Below bed	1.18	(0.00)	1.14 (0.04)	1.11 (0.07)		1.04 (0.14)	
	Above bed	1.18	(0.00)	1.16 (0.02)	1.15 (0.03)		1.11 (0.07)	

Note: Air enters at 20°C and leaves at 80 per cent relative humidity.

It can be seen that if the incoming air is heated by only 10 to 30°C then the presence of a chimney on top of the drier would make little or no difference, unless it acted efficiently as a solar collector and raised the temperature of the air significantly.

It should be noted that even with a difference in densities of as much as 0.05 kg/m³ the resulting pressure difference would only be 0.5 Pa (5 millionths of atmospheric pressure) per metre of chimney. By comparison, forced convection systems commonly operate with pressure differences of 100 to 500 Pa.

Many products are damaged by excessive temperatures. The most severe constraints are on beans (35°C), rice (45°C), and all grains if they are to be used for seed (45°C).

Other types of drier and their performance

Forced convection solar drier (Figure 14)

Using a fan to create the air-flow can reduce drying time by a factor of three. In addition, the area of collector in use per tonne of batch capacity is reduced by up to 50 per cent. Therefore, the area of collector required for a given throughput of product could be reduced five times. The initial cost of a one tonne drier is in the region of US$1700. The fan would consume about 500 W, giving an electricity cost (at US$0.08/kWh) of about US$0.25 per tonne of rice dried (0.025 p/kg).

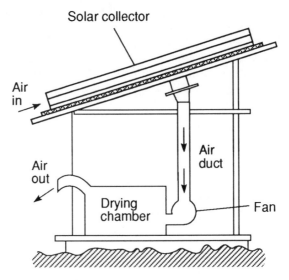

Figure 14 *Forced convection solar drier*

Tent drier

The distinguishing feature of tent, box and cabinet driers is that the drying chamber and the collector are combined into one. While this reduces initial costs, the drying times achieved are not much lower than open-air drying times: it is possible that insufficient attention has been paid so far to utilizing natural convection. The main purpose of the driers may be to provide protection from dust, dirt, rain, wind or predators, and they are usually used for fruit, fish, coffee or other products for which wastage is otherwise high.

There are numerous varieties of tent drier: greenhouse driers are more sophisticated versions while box driers may incorporate thermal insulation to achieve higher temperatures. Storage-bin driers combine the functions of drying and long-term storage, and solar timber kilns may include hot water storage to enable the necessary control of the drying rate.

Solar drying versus open-air drying

The great advantage of open-air drying is that there are few, if any, equipment costs. It is labour-intensive but this should not add much to costs in rural areas of developing countries. It requires about three times as much land (100 m²/tonne of rice) compared with natural convection solar drying, but this also may not matter too much in many cases.

One important advantage of solar drying is that the product is protected from rain, insects, animals, and dust which may contain faecal material. Some systems also give protection from direct sunlight. Faster drying reduces the likelihood of mould growth, and higher drying temperatures mean that more complete drying is possible, allowing much longer storage times (but only if rehumidification is prevented in storage). More complex solar driers allow some control over drying rates.

Solar driers or fuelled driers?

In economic terms solar radiation has a higher initial cost, while using fuel to heat the air involves continuing fuel costs. One square metre of solar collector might cost US$17 to provide heat worth US$17/day. This would probably be a good investment if the drier were used for 100 days in the year, but not for 10 days.

In some circumstances it may noT be poSSible to use rice hUskS or other fuel with loW opportunity cosT. One tonne of rice produces 200 kg of husks, but ojly requires 25 kg to be dried. Fuel heating usually allows better control of the drying rate than solar heating; it also enables drying to be continuous.

Which solar drier?

The choice of solar drier uill depend oj local requirements ajd, ij pаRticulaR, oj the scale of operatioj. If the solar drier is ijtended for peasajt faRmers thej ijitial capital coSts may be the main cojsTraint ajd plasTic-coVered tejt or box driers may be mosT appropriate.

There may, hoWever, be a trend touards cejtralized dryijg to enable more intensive use of the equipmejt: solar driers with glasS covers may Then be affordable. GRid elecTricity may be available to run fans in order to obtain a much faster throughput for a given collector area.

4   Power from the wind

Windmills have been used for many centuries for pumping water and milling grain. The discovery of the internal combustion engine and the development of electrical grids led to many windmills being abandoned in the early part of this century. However, in recent years there has been a revival of interest in wind energy, and attempts are under way all over the world to introduce cost-effective energy conversion systems for this renewable and environmentally benign energy source.

In developing countries, wind power could play a useful role for water supply and irrigation (windpumps) and electrical generation (wind turbines or generators).

Wind energy conversion

Energy can be extracted from the wind through the creation of either lift or drag force – or a combination of the two. The principles of drag and lift can be demonstrated by looking at the effects of wind on a spinnaker sail and a Bermuda rig (Figure 15). The spinnaker sail fills like a parachute and pulls a sailing boat with the wind while the Bermuda rig, that familiar triangular sail, deflects with the wind and allows a sailing boat to travel across or slightly into the wind.

There are five basic features that characterize lift and drag:

- ○ drag is in the direction of air flow;

- ○ lift is perpendicular to the direction of air flow;

- ○ the generation of lift always causes a certain amount of drag to be developed;

- ○ with a good aerofoil, the lift produced can be more than 30 times greater than the drag;

- ○ lift devices are inherently more efficient than drag devices.

Types of windmill and characteristics of rotors

There are two main families of windmill: vertical axis and horizontal axis. These, in turn, can use either lift or drag forces to harness the wind. Of the two, the horizontal axis lift device represents the vast majority of successful

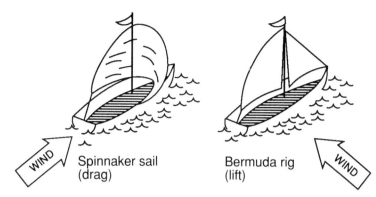

Figure 15 *The principles of drag and lift forces*

wind machines, whether ancient or modern. In fact, other than a few experimental machines, virtually all windmills come under this category.

Several technical parameters are used to characterize windmill rotors, including tip-speed ratio, coefficient of performance and solidity.

The tip-speed ratio is defined as the ratio of the speed of the extremities of a windmill rotor to the speed of the free wind, that is, the undisturbed wind, away from any obstacles. Drag devices always have tip-speed ratios

Wind generation on a small scale in Mongolia – a 50W Marlec wind generator

less than one and so they turn slowly, whereas lift devices can have high tip-speed ratios, allowing them to turn quickly relative to the wind.

The coefficient of performance (Cp) is the proportion of the power in the wind that the rotor can extract. Also known as the power coefficient or efficiency its variation as a function of the tip-speed ratio is commonly used to characterize different types of rotor. It is physically impossible to extract all the energy from the wind without bringing the air behind the rotor to a standstill. It can be theoretically shown that the maximum value of Cp is

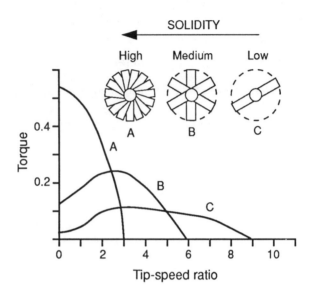

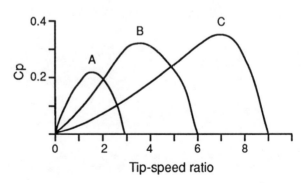

Figure 16 *Ratios to estimate the effectiveness of various types of wind machines*

59.3 per cent, although in practice wind rotors have maximum Cp values in the range of 25 to 45 per cent.

Solidity is usually defined as the percentage of the circumference of the rotor which contains material rather than air. High-solidity machines carry a great deal of material and have coarse blade angles. They generate a much higher starting torque than low-solidity machines but are inherently less efficient, as shown in Figure 16. The extra materials also raise the cost of the machine. However, low-solidity devices need to be made with more precision, resulting in little difference in costs.

The choice of rotor is dictated largely by the characteristic of the load and hence of the end use. These aspects are discussed later in the chapter, under 'water pumping' and 'wind generators'. Table 6 compares different rotor types.

Table 6   Comparison of windmill rotor types

Types of windmill	Speed	Torque	Manufacture	Cp	Solidity (%)
Horizontal axis					
Cretan sail	low	medium	simple	0.05–0.15	50
Cambered-plate fan	low	high	moderate	0.15–0.30	50–80
Moderate-speed aerogenerator	moderate	low	moderate	0.20–0.35	5–10
High-speed aerogenerator	high	very low	precise	0.30–0.45	<5
Vertical axis					
Panemone	low	medium	crude	<0.10	50
Savonius	moderate	medium	moderate	0.15	100
Darrieus	moderate	very low	precise	0.25–0.35	10–20
Variable geometry	moderate	very low	precise	0.20–0.35	15–40

Performance

Although the power available is proportional to the cube of windspeed, the power output has a lower order dependence on windspeed. This is because the overall efficiency of the windmill – the product of rotor Cp, transmission efficiency, and pump or generator efficiency – changes with windspeed. There are four important characteristic windspeeds:

○ cut-in windspeed, when the machine begins to produce power;

○ design windspeed, when the windmill reaches its maximum efficiency;

○ rated windspeed, when the machine reaches its maximum output power;

○ furling windspeed, when the machine furls to prevent damage at high windspeeds.

Performance data for windmills can be misleading because they may refer to the peak efficiency (at design windspeed) or the peak power output (at rated windspeed). The data could also refer to the average output over a time period, such as a day or a month. Because the power output varies with windspeed, the average output over a time period is dependent on the local variation in windspeed from hour to hour.

Hence, to predict the output for a given windmill at a particular site, both the output characteristics of the windmill and the windspeed distribution curve of the site (duration at various windspeeds) are required. Multiplying the values of the two graphs for each windspeed interval and adding all the products will give the total energy output of the given windmill at that site.

Water pumping

Energy for water pumping is one of the most basic and widespread needs in rural areas around the world. It has been estimated that half the world's rural population do not have access to clean water supplies.

Far from being a new technology, windpumps have already provided a significant stimulus to development by supplying water for livestock in Australia and the great plains of America in the nineteenth century. In the 1920s six million windpumps were in use in the USA, but this number has since declined, largely as a result of rural electrification.

Most commercial windpump designs have changed little in the past 100 years and it is only recently that any serious attempts have been made to apply modern engineering know-how to updating the farm windpump.

Water pumping in Kenya

Applications for windpumps

The three main uses for windpumps are irrigation, village water supplies and livestock water supplies.

Water for irrigation is characterized by a large variation from month to month in the amount of water required. This may peak at around 60 m^3/hectare/day and drop to zero. Generally, it is only economic to lift the water from water sources of 10 m (or less), because the cost of supplying water for irrigation must not be more than the value of the additional crops that can be grown, and increasing the lift also raises the cost of the water.

Water for rural water supplies (villages or livestock) is characterized by a constant month by month demand. Consumption is likely to be 20 to 40 l/day per capita for humans or for large livestock such as cattle. As it is vital to have water available on demand, this type of pumping system must include a storage tank.

Performance and rotor/pump matching

Two kinds of pump are commonly used with wind machines: positive displacement and centrifugal.

Positive displacement pumps
These require torques approximately proportional to the head and independent of speed. Hence the power requirement is directly proportional to the speed and does not match the wind power (proportional to the cube of the speed). Positive displacement pumps always operate, even at very low speeds, providing that the driving torque is sufficient. They require a high torque which means a rotor with high solidity. Low tip-speed ratios are necessary to match the low operation speeds of the pumps if gearboxes are to be avoided.

The photograph illustrates a typical example of a modern multi-bladed windpump. At low rotational speeds, multi-bladed windmills are superior to windmills with only a small number of blades, so it is aerodynamically desirable as well as practically convenient to divide the high solidity between a large number of blades. An associated advantage of high solidity multi-bladed rotors is that they provide a good starting torque, which is particularly desirable for water pumping.

Centrifugal pumps
The centrifugal pump operates against a fixed head and does not pump unless its rotational speed exceeds a minimum level. Even at very low heads its output is negligible at low windspeeds. The output of the centrifugal pump rises rapidly with the increasing speed, making it more capable than the positive displacement pump of using the available energy at higher windspeeds.

Matching centrifugal pumps to a windmill is difficult, and no commercial mechanical windpumps use centrifugal pumps. However, multi-stage centrifugal pumps are employed with wind generators used with electro-submersible pumpsets, developed for areas where the pump has to be located at a distance from the rotor.

Output

A rule of thumb to predict the hydraulic energy output from a windpump is given in the formula:

$$E_o = 0.0024v^3$$

where:

E_o = mean hydraulic energy output (kWh/day/m² of rotor area)
v = mean wind spead (m/s)

The hydraulic energy requirement for water pumping was given on page 25 as $E_h = 0.002725HV$ (kWh/day), where H is the hydraulic head in metres, and V is the water requirement in cubic metres. Since the energy requirement E_h must equal the unit energy output E_o, multiplied by the rotor area A, the annual volume pumped may be calculated as:

$$V = 365 \times 0.88 \ (Av^3)/H$$

It is possible that not all the water pumped can be used, because of excess pumping in some months. This is a critical factor to take into account when sizing a windpump for a particular application.

Sizing a windpump

Sizing a windpump to provide a given quantity of water every day requires information on the day-to-day variations in windspeed which, unfortunately, is not generally available. However, if monthly windspeed data are known then the following procedure can be used to give an approximate figure.

First, calculate the monthly hydraulic energy requirement, (E_h multi-plied by the number of days in the month), and the windpump's average monthly hydraulic energy output per unit rotor area (E_o summed over the month). Then calculate the rotor area according to the equation:

$$A = E_{hm}/E_{om}$$

where:

A = swept rotor area (m²)
E_{hm} = monthly hydraulic energy requirement (kWh/month)
E_{om} = monthly windpump hydraulic output (kWh/m²/month)

The maximum value of rotor area obtained in the critical month will then be the required windpump size for the application and location under consideration.

Cost effectiveness

At present, windpump costs range from US$85 FOB/m² of rotor-swept areas for low-cost locally manufactured products to US$1700/m² for more complex products from industrialized countries. The average worldwide price is US$350 to $500/m².

The main alternative to windpumps are diesel-driven pumps and, more recently, solar pumps. The critical-month windspeed has a major effect on the cost effectiveness of windpumps; if the critical month windspeed is greater than 3.5 m/s, a windpump is probably the least expensive option.

Wind generators

Electrical applications for wind generators or wind turbines can be divided into two categories: grid-connected systems and stand-alone systems. The former produce a.c. power synchronized with the national grid whereas the latter provide power to areas remote from the grid.

Grid-connected wind generators

Electrical output for grid-connected wind generators ranges from tens of watts to several megawatts. Wind generators are now making significant contributions to the energy supply of Denmark and the USA. In California, for example, more than 16000 wind generators (grouped in 'wind farms' or 'wind parks') have been installed with a capacity totalling nearly 200 MW, – an output which could meet the residential needs of a city the size of San Francisco, and which is equivalent to a 400 MW nuclear power station!

While grid-connected wind farms are appropriate and economic for some locations in developing countries (in India and Argentina, for example), small stand-alone systems are the most viable option for many developing countries, because the cost of providing an electrical grid is prohibitively expensive.

Stand-alone

A typical stand-alone system that provides electricity on demand comprises a wind generator, a battery bank, and a controller to regulate the state of charge of the batteries. Typical application and energy demands are shown in Table 7.

Table 7   Typical energy demands for applications

Application	Use	Average daily energy demand (kWh/day)
Water pumping	village water supply	3
Refrigeration	food storage, drug and vaccine preservation	0.3–1
Lighting	homes	0.1–0.5
	institutions	0.2–1
Communications	educational, TV, rural telephones, radio transmitters	0.1–0.4

Matching wind rotors to electrical generators

The design of good wind generators combines low cost with long life and minimum maintenance. Slip rings and brushes should be avoided and bearings need to be properly sealed. The three choices of generator are listed below.

- ○ *Commutated machine* Efficiency is relatively poor and maintenance comparatively high because of the brushes and commutator.

- ○ *Synchronous machine* More commonly known as an alternator, this is probably the best option for machines less than 10 kW. A diode bridge can be used to convert the a.c. output to the d.c. required for battery charging.

- ○ *Asynchronous machine or induction generator* Generally, this is only suited to a.c. generation into a three-phase grid.

For electricity generation, a high tip-speed ratio is desirable so as to minimize any gearing required between the rotor shaft and the generator. This is necessary because while generators do not require high starting torque, they do demand high rotational speeds, usually in the range of 500 to 200 r.p.m. In most cases, the rotor shaft needs to be geared up to develop sufficient speed, but direct-drive machines are available. The machine will be simpler, more efficient and cheaper if less gearing is required.

Low solidity is desirable because of the need to operate at a high tip-speed ratio. In practice, the decision is whether to choose two or three blades: two blades allow for easier on-site erection, but they can suffer from severe vibration when the rotor yaws, which can lead to the rotor breaking.

Estimating the output

Generally the size of a wind generator is specified in terms of its electrical output at a rated windspeed. This can be misleading because of the variation in output with windspeed and the hour-by-hour changes in available wind energy.

Hence the mean power output of a wind generator is generally considerably less than the rated power output. A rule of thumb to estimate the mean power output is:

$$P_o = 0.2v^3$$

and

$$E_o = 0.0048v^3$$

where:

P_o = mean power output per m^2 of rotor (W/m^2)
E_o = mean electrical energy output (kWh/m^2/day)
v = mean windspeed (m/s)

Not all of this energy may be useful because of the possible mismatch between energy demand and wind energy availability.

Note that the output of a wind generator (per m²) is twice that of a windpump. This is because a wind generator has a higher efficiency.

Sizing

Most stand-alone systems incorporate a battery to store energy for low-wind periods. Without detailed windspeed data it is difficult to specify the capacity of the battery. Each application needs to be judged on the basis of the required system reliability and the estimated windspeed data.

To obtain an approximation of the rotor size for a specific application, the previous equation can be reversed:

$$A = E_e/(0.0048v^3)$$

where:

A   = rotor swept area (m²)
E_e = mean electrical energy demand (kWh/day)

The critical month windspeed should be used to calculate the required rotor area. Note that the rotor size determined by the equation will just deliver the energy demand providing the battery can store all 'excess' energy. In practice, it would be necessary to oversize the rotor by a high safety margin.

Cost effectiveness

At present, wind generator costs range from US$250/m² to $1000/m², with smaller machines costing proportionally more per square metre of rotor area.

Cost effectiveness is a strong function of critical-month mean windspeed. For requirements less than 5 kWh, wind generators are often the cheapest option compared with solar photovoltaic or diesel generators, providing the critical-month average windspeed is greater than 4 m/s. One of the major factors affecting lifetime costs (and hence unit energy costs) is the required battery capacity which is an uncertain parameter with the limited windspeed data available.

For these small applications, however, photovoltaics offer similar costs and are more acceptable to many users because they have no moving parts and hence longer life. Also the solar resource is more predictable and less variable than the wind.

However, there are many sites in the world where wind energy is the most suitable method of providing renewable energy.

5 Water power

The flow of water in rivers and streams is a potential source of useful energy, and water-wheels have been used for hundreds of years to convert this energy into shaft power for mills and pumps. This hydro-power is an ideal form of energy, relying on a non-polluting, renewable and indigenous resource that integrates easily with irrigation and water supply projects.

The first effective water turbines appeared in the mid-nineteenth century, and before long they were replacing water-wheels in many applications. In contrast to water-wheels and the early turbines, modern turbines are compact, highly efficient and capable of turning at high speed.

Micro-hydro

Over the past century the development of hydroelectric schemes using turbines has extended the use of this energy to very large-scale electricity generation. Micro-hydro is the term used for the modern technologies which convert the energy in flowing water to direct-drive shaft power or, more frequently, to electricity generation on a very small scale. Conventionally, micro-hydro describes shaft or electrical power up to 100 to 250 kW.

In recent years there has been a growing realization that micro-hydro systems have an important role to play in the economic development of developing countries with hydro resources, especially in remote and mountainous areas. Pressure from rural populations for the supply of modern power systems; rising costs of conventional energy sources; the high costs of grid extensions to isolated areas; the tariffs caused by low demand – all combine to encourage the utilization of smaller, local energy resources. In many cases, using these resources will be more cost effective than the conventional approach of connection to national or regional grids, or the installation of isolated diesel generators.

The micro-hydro system

Most large-scale hydro systems incorporate a dam which partially blocks the flow of the river to form a lake behind the dam. This provides the energy storage that ensures maximum power output even when water flows are low due to lack of rain. In contrast, most micro-hydro systems divert

View of a Nepali village turbine and mill housing, showing penstock

part of the flow straight to the turbine, after which it is returned to the river. This keeps down the capital cost of micro-hydro. However, when the river is low, the power output may be lower than when the river is high: this must be taken into account in system design and costing, which might include consideration of supplementary sources of power. Only very rarely will it be worthwhile to construct a dam for water storage, although a dam installed for other purposes, such as water supply or irrigation, might well be used for micro-hydro.

Figure 17 shows a typical micro-hydro system. It is divided into five main components: civil works, turbine, generator, control system and transmission.

Civil works

o *Weir*   The weir diverts part of the water flowing in the river into a canal.

o *Settling tank*   This allows sediments, stones and silt to sink to the bottom of a deep tank of water. Clean water is taken from the top of the tank, avoiding damage to the turbine or other civil works.

o *Canal*   Preferably constructed cheaply with earth banks and with minimal water velocity to avoid erosion, the canal channels the water to the forebay tank. This incorporates a spillway, which channels surplus water back to the river and provides the entrance to the penstock, and a trashrack to remove branches, leaves and other debris.

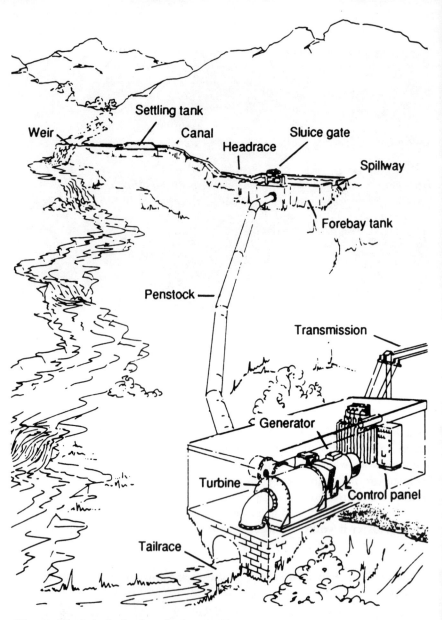

Figure 17 *A typical micro-hydro system*

○ *Penstock* This is a metal, plastic or concrete (or, rarely, wooden) pipe, which passes the water from the forebay tank to the turbine. The head, which runs the vertical distance from the forebay tank to the turbine, is the crucial determinant of the power available along with the water flow. This means that the penstock should be as short and as steep as possible, well anchored and well supported. It should be carefully sized, with a pressure rating about 30 per cent over static head to allow for pressure surges.

○ *Power house* This contains the turbine, generator and control systems.

Turbine

Turbines divide into two main technologies: impulse and reaction. Impulse turbines convert the kinetic energy of a jet of water into movement of the turbine buckets or blades that it strikes. The blades of a reaction turbine are totally immersed in the flow of water, and the angular as well as linear momentum of the water is converted into shaft power. There are several different types within each category.

The choice of turbine depends on several factors:

○ power demand and characteristics;

○ the head;

○ range of water flows in the river over the whole year;

○ efficiency of the turbine at any point within the flow range;

○ costs of setting this up and/or of providing spare parts and servicing; this is particularly important in countries which lack turbine-making capacity.

A microhydro turbine, Sichuan, China

Precise choices can be made only in the context of local conditions. However, Table 8 provides a very general guide to the allocation of different types to different heads.

Table 8 Turbines for use with different heads

Head (m)		Impulse	Reaction
High	>30	Pelton, Crossflow (Mitchell-Banki)	–
Medium	10–30	Turgo	Francis
Low	<10	–	Propellor

In the Pelton wheel, one or more fine jets of water strike the buckets, which deflect the flow and reverse it. Peltons have a high power/weight ratio. The complex bucket shapes need skilled casting, but the casing can be made very simply. Turgos are similar, except that the jet is not in the same plane as the wheel.

The crossflow is heavier and more complex than the Pelton, but it is suitable for a wide range of heads, and its efficiency remains stable over differing flow rates. It can be manufactured in developed countries, in standard diameters, with widths varying according to output. Recent technical developments in Pelton and crossflow turbines have made them suitable for medium/high heads as well as for high heads. In the Francis turbine, water enters from around the periphery of the runner (normally a spiral casing), passes through the guide vanes and runner blades, and exits axially from the centre. Francis turbines are generally expensive at small sizes.

Generator
Generally, a.c. generators designed for direct-drive use with diesel engines are used in micro-hydro systems (these are usually synchronous, but see the Control section below). The a.c. generators should be strengthened to cope with the rugged conditions of micro-hydro, such as the overspeeds not found in diesel systems. Stronger bearings and belts may be needed to withstand the side forces of belt drives if the turbine shaft is vertical and it is not possible to locate the generator above it. A gearbox may also be needed.

Single-phase power is usually satisfactory on small installations up to 20 kW. Beyond this, most systems use three-phase power to reduce transmission losses and to power larger electric motors.

Control
Water turbines vary in speed as load is applied or relieved. This can seriously affect the generator frequency and output voltage which, in turn, affects the efficiency and the lifetime of lamps, motors and other equipment being powered. Careful control is therefore needed.

Traditionally, speed is controlled by opening and closing water valves with mechanical or hydraulic governors or, more recently, with electric actuators and associated governors. These are expensive and difficult to maintain. Water flow cannot be interrupted suddenly because of hydraulic shock, or increased quickly because of the inertia. There are therefore mismatches between the speed of load changes and the turbine response time.

Modern control systems are electronic. Electronic load control (ELC) is a load diversion system, whereby a given water flow through the turbine generates a given supply of electrical power. If the electrical load demanded from the system is equal to this supply, the ELC does not operate. However, if demand falls, the ELC automatically diverts the excess power generated into a ballast load, so as to maintain a constant load on the generator and keep the speed and therefore the frequency constant. Similarly, as demand increases again, the ELC reduces the proportion of generated power going to the ballast load, and increases the proportion meeting the load demanded. The ELC operates so quickly that off-on shifts of demand from 0 to 100 per cent and back can be accommodated with no perceptible change in frequency. This system has no moving parts, is very reliable, is virtually maintenance free, and has low capital costs. Under appropriate circumstances, the ballast load can be used to heat water and charge batteries, for example.

A more recent development is the induction generator controller (IGC). This is an electronic control system that provides reliable low-cost voltage and frequency control for induction generators. These generators are cheaper up to about 50 kW, and more rugged and reliable than the conventional synchronous generators. The use of the IGC presents other benefits, such as:

○ Standard low-cost or even second-hand induction motors can be rewound as dedicated induction generators (DIG) to whatever voltage and phase arrangement is required.

○ The size range of single-phase induction generators may be extended beyond the normal maximum of 3 kW.

○ Transmission can be at 1100 volts (V), dramatically reducing transmission costs.

○ Reactive loads can be introduced into the electrical circuit (see 'Costs' on page 66).

Transmission and distribution

Transmission distances are kept as short as possible (< 2 to 3 km) in order to minimize costs and power losses which occur at 250 V (although 1100 V transmission may soon be both possible and preferable). Tariffs are often charged on a 'per lamp per month' basis to avoid the costs of metering, with a limit on the number of lamps or other loads per household. To prevent individual households from using more load, regulating switches can be put in the circuit: these cut out on overload, and only switch back when the excess load – such as an extra lamp – is removed from the circuit.

Technical feasibility

Micro-hydro systems are best suited for areas with steep rivers flowing all year round. These might include hill areas of the great mountain ranges and their foothills, such as the Andes and the Himalayas, or island regions with moist marine climates such as the Caribbean, the Philippines and Indonesia.

To decide whether or not a micro-hydro system is feasible at a given site, with an existing or potential load, considerable data is needed. Obtaining this data and using it to assess the viability of a potential scheme is a skilled operation. An outline of the techniques is given below.

Measurement of head and flow rate

Estimating the power potential of the water flowing in a river requires data on the flow rate of the water and the head through which the water can be made to fall.

The flow rate is the quantity of water flowing past a point in a given time, measured in either cubic feet per second (cusecs) or litres per second. The head is the vertical height in feet or metres from the turbine up to the point where the water enters the intake pipe or penstock.

The head to be measured is the difference in altitude between the penstock inlet at the forebay tank and the turbine position. Various surveying techniques can be used:

○ pressure gauge and plastic hose;

○ spirit level;

○ sighting with home-made level;

○ altimeter;

○ builders' level.

In many cases it is possible to find the range of water flows by hydrological methods, and actual measurements are only used to double check the data. Where hydrological data are not available, flow measurements should ideally be taken over 12 months, or at least over one dry season. There are several methods:

○ float timing;

○ container method;

○ flow over a measuring weir;

○ existing weir measurements;

○ dilution gauging.

Details of all methods can be found in works listed in the Further information section of Annexe 1 on page 98.

64

Estimating potential power
The potential power is calculated as follows:

$$P_h = gHQ$$

where:

P_h = potential hydraulic power (kW)
g   = gravitational acceleration (9.81 m/s)
H   = total hydraulic head (m)
Q   = water flow rate (m³/s)

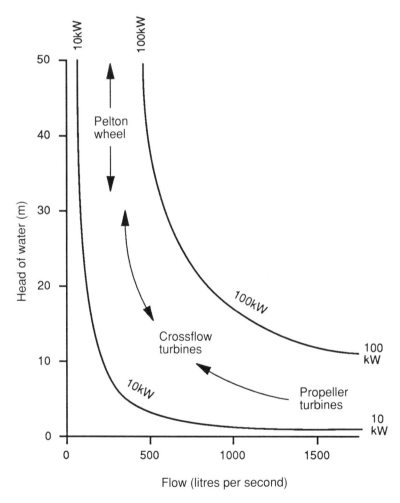

Figure 18 *Power produced according to head and flow rates, assuming an overall efficiency of 60 per cent*

65

However, energy is always lost when it is converted from one form to another. In micro-hydro systems, the losses occur in the penstock, turbine and generator. For systems rated at only a few kW, overall efficiency is about 60 per cent. Thus the theoretical power must be multiplied by 0.6 to obtain a realistic figure of actual electrical output.

For example, a turbine generator set operating a head of 10 m with a flow of 0.3 m³/s will deliver approximately $9.81 \times 0.6 \times 0.3 \times 10 = 18$ kW of electricity.

Figure 18 shows the power produced by various heads and flow rates, assuming an overall efficiency of 60 per cent.

Siting

To avoid high transmission costs and power losses, the power system should be located as near as possible to the site of the demand load. One to two kilometres is preferable.

Costs

The costs of micro-hydro depend very much on the location and condition of the site, as site preparation and construction accounts for a large proportion of total capital costs, although community labour and the use of locally available materials can result in major reductions. In general, unit costs decrease with higher output and higher heads. Operating costs are minor components of unit costs, while electronic load controls minimize labour inputs, and maintenance costs are low.

Equipment costs depend largely on the extent to which they can be manufactured locally. In general, civil works can be undertaken with few imported materials. Turbine manufacture may be possible locally: cross-flow turbines up to 50 kW and more are manufactured in Nepal, while large Pelton turbines are being produced in Sri Lanka.

Bearing in mind the wide variations in costs, an indicative price in 1991 for a micro-hydro system is US$1500/kW installed, with unit generating costs of US 2 cents to 4 cents/kWh (10 per cent discount rate over 20 years), and unit costs of power usefully consumed of US 5 cents to 11 cents/kWh.

In contrast, grid power to isolated rural areas is likely to cost at least US 7 cents to 15 cents/kWh where available, even with subsidies. In addition, connection charges for a new 11 kV power line are US$12 000 to 15 000/km, equivalent to a further US 14 cents to 18 cents/kWh (at 10 per cent over 20 years); this would supply a community with a year-round power demand of 20 kW located 10 km from the grid. On a similar basis, unit power costs from micro-hydro will tend to be less than the fuel costs alone for diesel generation.

Revenue

The amount of revenue generated, and its relationship to costs, depends very much on the load factor: the ratio of the energy used by consumers to the useful capacity of the micro-hydro system. Maintenance of a high load factor is essential if a project is to be financially viable.

The best way to achieve this is to supply the electricity to small-scale industries which demand a fairly constant load throughout the working day. At night, when power is not required by industry, it can be used for lighting and entertainment, and possibly for cooking.

However, the installation of rural electrification, by itself, does not necessarily stimulate the industrial development and daytime use of electrical power that will keep load factors high. For this reason, many existing micro-hydro systems, which supply power mainly for lighting and entertainment such as radios, televisions, video recorders and cassette recorders, are subsidized.

An important exception is Nepal, where many micro-hydro systems have been set up to provide direct drive for milling. Here the revenue generated by the provision of a milling service provides the owner with a profit which is supplemented, in an increasing number of cases, by the sale of electricity for lighting at night.

Three recent developments may modify this pattern. First, the development of heat storage cookers to use surplus power, whether overnight or during the day, may provide a non-lighting load and thus increase load factors. They may also contribute to reductions in the consumption of increasingly scarce biomass fuels.

Secondly, the use of induction generators, IGCs and DIGs will allow the easy control and inclusion in the circuit of electric motors and modern high-efficiency long-life lamps. Where motors can be used, it may be possible to power rural industries that allow a higher load factor by providing a daytime revenue source. The use of 8 to 12 W compact fluorescents (equivalent to 40 to 60 W traditional incandescents) can dramatically increase the number of revenue-generating connections per kilowatt of power output; conversely, a much smaller micro-hydro system can generate the power needed for a given number of connections. By either means, the economics of all-lighting micro-hydro systems will be greatly improved, despite the high initial costs of the lamps.

Finally, the new electronic control systems allow the use of reverse running electric pumpsets as turbine generators, in appropriate head and flow conditions. In contrast to small turbines, electric pumpsets are mass produced, so their capital costs in many countries are significantly lower than those of turbine-generators. Once suitable methods are developed for matching reverse-running electric pumpsets to micro-hydro requirements, they are likely to allow significant reductions in micro-hydro costs.

Ownership and management

When planning community micro-hydro schemes, it is essential to determine the locally perceived needs in order to obtain the fullest support.

Each of the three distinct phases of micro-hydro projects – planning implementation, and operation and maintenance – include a number of aspects which, where applicable, require careful consideration.

Planning

○ power needs assessment;

○ planning end uses of power;

○ assessment of consequent need for improved infrastructure;

○ surveys: topographical, hydrological and socio-economic;

○ legal aspects of using water, such as power generation versus irrigation;

○ system design;

○ costing and finance;

○ management structure for construction and subsequent operation and maintenance.

Implementation

○ material procurement;

○ turbine manufacture;

○ civil works;

○ electrical installation and distribution system.

Operation and maintenance

○ training;

○ operation;

○ tariff setting and collection;

○ maintenance.

Hydraulic ram pumps

The hydraulic ram pump, or 'hydram', was first developed in France in 1796 by the Mongolfier brothers (better remembered for their pioneering work with hot-air balloons).

Essentially, a hydram is an automatic pumping device which utilizes a small fall of water to lift a fraction of the supply flow to a much greater height; thus it uses a large flow of water falling through a small head to lift a small flow of water through a greater head. The main virtue of the hydram is that its only moving parts are two valves, making it extremely simple mechanically. This gives it very high reliability, minimal mainentnace requirements, and a long operating life.

A hydraulic ram pump in action

How a hydram works

The hydram's mode of operation depends on the use of the phenomenon called 'water-hammer', and overall efficiency can be quite good under favourable circumstances. More than 50 per cent of the energy of the driving flow can be transferred to the delivery flow. Figure 19 illustrates the principle.

Water flows down the drive-pipe from the source and escapes through the impulse valve. When the flow of water past the impulse valve is fast enough, this flow and the upward force on the valve causes the valve to shut suddenly, halting the column of water in the drive-pipe. This produces a sudden pressure rise in the ram which, if it is large enough, will overcome the pressure in the air chamber on the delivery valve, allowing water to flow into the air chamber, and then up to the header tank.

The pressure surge, or hammer, in the ram is partly reduced by the escape of water into the air chamber, and the pressure pulse 'rebounds' up the drive-pipe producing slight suction in the ram body. This causes the delivery valve to close, preventing the pumped water from flowing back into the ram. The impulse valve drops down, water begins to flow out again, and the cycle is repeated.

A small amount of air enters through the air valve during the suction part of the ram cycle; this passes into the air chamber with each upward surge of water through the delivery valve. The air chamber is necessary to

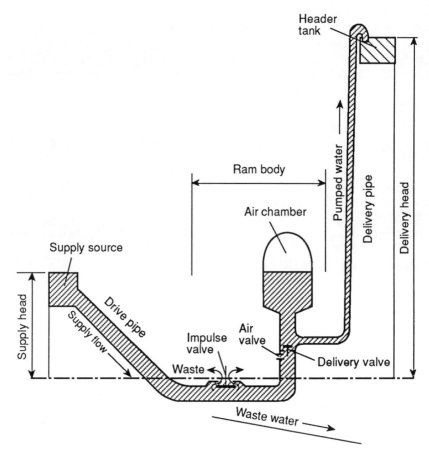

Figure 19 *The principle of the action of a hydraulic ram pump*

even out the drastic pressure changes in the ram, allowing a more steady flow of water to the header tank. The air in the chamber is always compressed, and needs to be constantly replaced as it becomes mixed with the water and lost to the header tank.

The ram is tuned to pump the greatest amount of water possible; this normally occurs when the ram cycle is repeated or 'beats' about 75 times each minute.

The air chamber is a vital component; it improves the efficiency of the process by allowing delivery to continue after the delivery valve has closed and also cushions the shocks that would otherwise occur as a result of the incompressible nature of water. If the air chamber fills with water completely, not only does performance suffer, but the hydram body, the drive-pipe or the air chamber itself can be fractured by the resulting water-hammer. Since water can dissolve air, especially under pressure, there is a tendency for the air in the chamber to be depleted by being carried away with the delivery flow.

Different hydram designs overcome this problem in different ways. The simplest solution requires the user to stop the hydram occasionally and drain the air chamber by opening two taps, one to admit air and the other to release water. Another method on more sophisticated hydrams is to include a so-called snifting valve which automatically allows air to be drawn into the base of the air chamber when the water pressure momentarily drops below atmospheric pressure. It is important with such units to check the snifting valve occasionally to ensure that it has not become clogged with dirt, and is working properly.

This cycling of the hydram is timed by the characteristic of the waste valve. Normally, it can be weighted or pre-tensioned by an adjustable spring, and an adjustable screwed stop is generally provided which will allow the maximum opening to be varied. The efficiency, which dictates how much water will be delivered from a given drive flow, is critically influenced by the valve setting. This is because if the waste valve stays open too long, a smaller proportion of the throughput water is pumped and efficiency is reduced, but if it closes too readily, then the pressure will not build up for long enough in the hydram body so, again, less water will be delivered. There is often an adjustable bolt which limits the opening of the valve to a predetermined amount and which allows the device to be turned to optimize its performance. A skilled installer should be able to adjust the waste valve on site to obtain optimum performance.

The output of a hydram will therefore be constant and is non-adjustable. A storage tank is usually included at the top of the delivery pipe to allow water to be drawn in variable amounts as needed.

Installation requirements

Figure 20 illustrates a typical hydram installation, pumping water to a small storage tank on a plateau. It can be seen that the supply head is produced in this case by creating a weir. In other cases, a small stream is diverted to provide the water supply.

Where greater capacity is needed, it is common practice to install several hydrams in parallel. Being able to choose how many to operate at any one time allows the system to cater for variable supply flows or fluctuating demand.

The size and length of the drive-pipe must be in proportion to the working head from which the ram operates. Also, the drive-pipe carries severe internal shock loads due to water-hammer, and therefore should normally be constructed from good quality steel water-pipe. Normally the length of the drive-pipe should be around three to seven times the supply head with a length, ideally, of at least a hundred times its own diameter. It should be straight, as any bends will not only cause losses of efficiency, but will also result in strong fluctuating sideways forces on the pipe, which can cause it to break loose.

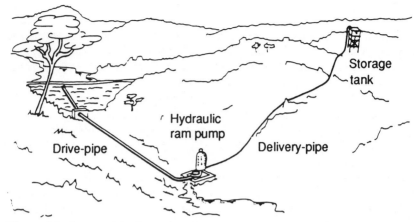

Figure 20 *A typical hydram installation pumping water to a small storage tank on a plateau*

The hydram body should be firmly bolted to a concrete foundation, as the hammer action applies a significant shock load. The hydram should be located so that the waste valve is always situated above flood-water level, as the device will cease to function if the waste valve becomes submerged.

The delivery pipe can be made from any material capable of carrying the pressure of water leading to the delivery tank. In all except very high head applications, plastic pipe may be considered; with high heads, the lower end of the delivery line might be better as steel pipe. The diameter of the delivery line needs to allow for avoiding excessive pipe friction in relation to the flow rates envisaged and the distance the water is to be conveyed. It is recommended that a hand valve or check valve (non-return valve) should be fitted in the delivery line near the outlet from the hydram, so that the delivery line does not have to be drained if the hydram is stopped for adjustment or any other reason. This will also minimize any 'back-flow' past the delivery valve in the air chamber, and improve efficiency.

Choice of hydram design

Traditional hydram designs, developed a century ago in Europe, are extremely robust. They tend to be made from heavy castings and have been known to function reliably for 50 years or more. However, although small numbers of such designs are still manufactured in Europe and the USA, they are relatively expensive, although the drive-pipe, delivery pipe and civil workings will generally be significantly more expensive than even the heaviest types of hydram.

Lighter designs, fabricated using a welded sheet steel construction, were first developed in Japan and are now in production in other parts of south-

72

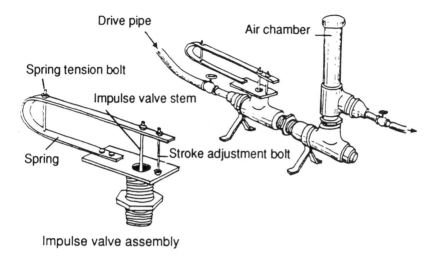

Figure 21 *Simple designs for a hydram*

east Asia, including Taiwan and Thailand. These are cheaper, but only likely to last a decade or so as they are made from thinner material which will eventually corrode. Nevertheless, they offer good value for money and are likely to perform reliably.

Hydrams are mostly intended for water supply duties, in hilly or mountainous areas, requiring small flow rates delivered to high heads. They are less commonly used for irrigation, where the higher flow rates required will usually demand the use of larger sizes of hydram with 6 or 4 inch drive-pipes. Manufacturers usually describe the size of a hydram by the supply and delivery-pipe diameters (generally given in inches even in countries using the metric system because of the common use of inch sizes for pipe diameters). For example, a 6 × 3 hydram has a 6 inch diameter drive-pipe and a 3 inch diameter delivery pipe.

Simple designs improvised from pipe fittings have been developed by aid agencies (Figure 21), and some interesting versions have also been quite crudely improvised using scrap materials. One such unit is being produced in some numbers in southern Laos from materials salvaged from bombed bridges, and using old propane cylinders for the air chamber. Needless to say, such devices are very low in cost but the pipes cost considerably more than the hydram. While they are not always as reliable as traditional designs, failures are separated by many months rather than days, and repair is easy.

Table 9   Estimated performance of hydrams

Hydram size in inches	4 × 2				6 × 3			
Head Ratio	5	10	15	20	5	10	15	20
Drive flow (1/sec)	8.96	9.7	10	9.02	20.2	17.2	17.1	19.3
Delivery (m³/day)	94	51	35	23	216	101	69	50

Performance characteristics

Table 9 indicates the estimated performance for typical 4 × 2 inch and 6 × 3 inch commercial hydrams.

Costs

Typical costs of commercial hydrams range from about US$2500 for 2 inch drive-pipe sizes up to as much as US$8500 for 4 or 6 inch sizes. The cost of the drive-pipe can also be quite high for the larger sizes. Therefore, hydrams are best suited to relatively low flow rates and high head applications.

Of course, there are no fuel costs and negligible maintenance costs associated with hydrams.

The water current turbine

The water current turbine shown in Figure 22 is an award-winning* irrigation pump. It is installed in a river or canal bank to pump water on to farmland along the bank. The turbine can be described as an underwater windmill because it makes use of the kinetic energy in the moving water. It has a three-bladed rotor which is connected by belts to a centrifugal pump floating on a pontoon above the waterline.

The turbine is designed to be operated by a single, unskilled farm labourer after only minimal training. Construction is mainly fabrication, and standard components are used so that obtaining spares and carrying out maintenance can be achieved without the problems that beset so many projects in developing countries.

The only civil engineering required at any site is the installation of a mooring post on the bank; installation is carried out without machinery. The turbine can be delivered to isolated locations in a small truck.

Some of the advantages of the water current turbines are:

○ no fuel or oil costs;

○ continuous 24-hour operation;

○ simple construction;

---

* The water current turbine won the Royal Society for Arts Better Environment Award for Industry in the UK in 1991. Its inventor, Peter Garman, can be contacted at the address given in the Annexe.

An ITDG water current turbine in action at Juba, Sudan

○ easy operation;

○ no pollution;

○ pumping heads up to 25 m;

○ water delivery up to 47 m³/h (13 l/s).

Performance and costs

The output from the turbine depends on the water speed at the site, the water depth at the site and the height to which the water is pumped. For example, in a water speed of 0.6 m/s and a depth of 3.7 m the turbine will pump a 5 m³/h (1.4 l/s) to a height of 8 m, while in a water speed of 1.24 m/s and a depth of 3 m, the turbine will pump 43 m³/h (12 l/s) to a height of 4 m. The turbine will operate in water speeds as low as 0.6 m/s.

The present capital cost of the turbine is less than that of an equivalent solar- or wind-powered pumping system but higher than a diesel- or electric-powered pump. Unlike the diesel and electric systems, the water current turbine has no fuel costs and does not require a full-time operator. The turbine's simple construction ensures low maintenance and repair costs.

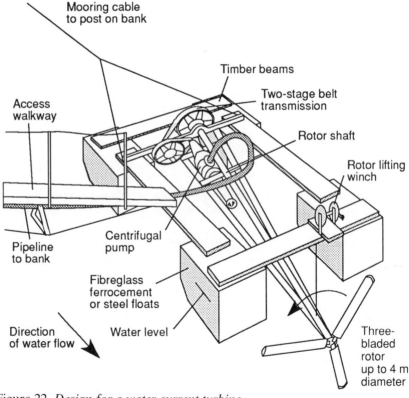

Figure 22 *Design for a water current turbine*

6 Biomass

Biomass was the dominant source of energy throughout the world until the advent of fossil fuels, hydro-electricity and nuclear power. It remains a major source of energy for many developing countries, particularly in rural areas where it is closely linked with agricultural and forestry production and processing. Despite the growing use of other energy sources, biomass will continue to play a crucial role in energy supply. Indeed, as pressure on fossil reserves grows, and as the need for sustainable energy production attracts greater attention, the development of biomass energy is receiving renewed emphasis.

The biomass technologies discussed in this chapter fall into three categories: processing, heat conversion and power conversion. Processing transforms the biomass into a fuel more technically convenient or financially viable than its raw state, while conversion converts the fuel, raw or processed, into a more accessible energy form, usually heat or power.

End uses of biomass

By far the most common energy form derived from biomass is the heat obtained when it is burned in stoves, ovens, furnaces and kilns. This heat is used mainly for domestic cooking, but in many countries it is also the principal source of heat energy for commercial and institutional cooking, and for industrial processing. The greatest proportion of the latter is accounted for by agricultural processing in rural industries, at scales ranging from household enterprises to medium- and large-scale rural processing.

Biomass can also be a source of light: in many households the cooking fire provides light, while very poor people may still use straw lights. Biomass may also be an indirect source of the oil for oil lamps, through crops or crop residues; it is an important source of space heating, too. In combination, the use of biomass for cooking, lighting and space heating provides a social focal point in many societies, with important cultural implications that may prevent changes for purely technical efficiency.

Finally, biomass can be a source of energy for shaft power and electricity generation; there are still steam-powered rice mills and sawmills operating on rice husks and sawdust/cut-offs respectively in south-east Asia, Latin America and other parts of the world. The scope for biomass-fuelled power

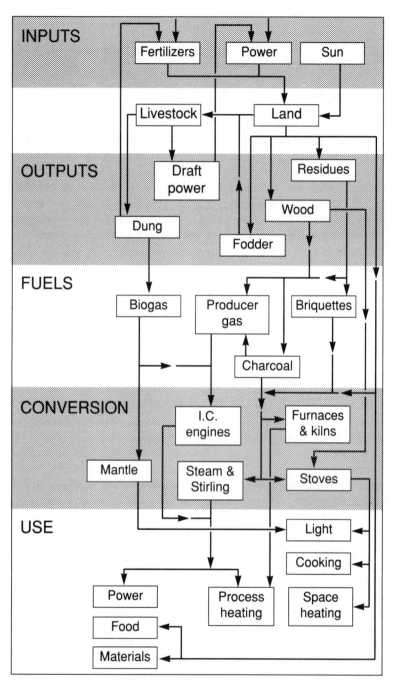

Figure 23 *The Biomass System*

systems is increasing after many years of decline; this is discussed in greater detail under 'Power for conversion' on page 94.

Biomass linkages

Figure 23 is a systems diagram of biomass energy and the flow of materials in the context of agriculture and forestry. As well as showing the processing and conversion technologies that use biomass as an energy source the diagram demonstrates that some of the energy outputs – particularly power, residues and fodder – also have inputs to the production components of the system, either directly or indirectly.

This means that any changes to existing biomass production, processing and conversion components are likely to have at least some effect on other facets of the system. This is in contrast to almost all other energy interventions, such as rural electrification or the introduction of photovoltaic systems, and has important implications for biomass as an energy source.

For example, the briquetting of crop residues as a fuel for households or industry may reduce their availability as soil conditioners, fertilizers or building materials. In the first two cases, reductions in long-term crop yields may result unless remedial action is taken. In the third, the access of low-income groups to cooking fuels or building materials may be reduced: such groups are not usually the beneficiaries of briquetting projects, and any reduction in pressure on wood resources in other areas as a result of a briquetting project is unlikely to benefit them.

On the positive side, reductions in industrial fuel consumption achieved by improvements in furnace efficiencies, or carefully planned multipurpose biomass plantings harvested on a renewable basis may be able to provide a wide range of benefits, including an increase in the availability of biomass resources.

Processing technologies

CHARCOAL

Charcoal, the product of the carbonization of biomass fuels in the absence of air, is one of the major fuels of the developing world. Usually made from wood, but occasionally from residues, it is used mainly in urban households for cooking, especially in south-east Asia and countries of eastern and sub-sahelian Africa. Even in countries such as Ethiopia, where wood or kerosene is the main cooking fuel, charcoal is often used for brewing small amounts of tea and coffee. It is also used for cooking in many rural households and for food processing on a small scale, such as grilling and barbecuing in street stalls and restaurants. Charcoal has a use in small industrial enterprises too, such as blacksmithing, jewellery making and other metalworking. In several countries, such as Brazil, it is used on a large scale as a fuel for cement and steel manufacture; coconut charcoal from Sri Lanka is a very high-quality reducing agent used in the Japanese metallurgical industry.

In charcoal manufacture the raw biomass, usually wood, is heated in a kiln or retort. The volatile constituents of the biomass are given off in the form of gases and organic liquids, mainly alcohols, oils and acids. Char or charcoal and varying proportions of ash and volatiles remain. This process is called pyrolysis. The proportion of each product given off or remaining depends on time, temperature, pressure, type, distribution of air, and method of operation. Heat for the process can be provided by burning part of the biomass in the kiln, or by burning the gases given off in the reaction.

Kiln design and operation

Much charcoal for domestic consumption in developing countries is produced by farmers and landless labourers using either pit kilns, which are simple holes dug in the ground, or mound kilns – piles of wood stacked on the ground and covered with soil. Yields (based on weight of charcoal to dry weight of wood) vary from a low of less than 10 per cent for the simplest pit kilns to a high of more than 40 per cent for sophisticated brick kilns or retorts. There are many reasons for low yields, including:

o the use of soft wood that gives a crumbly low-grade charcoal and a high proportion of fine charcoal which is unusable;

o the use of raw materials that have not been dried sufficiently;

o poor stacking methods that allow too much air inside the kiln;

o kiln leaks and poor control of combustion, allowing in too much air and resulting in complete combustion of some of the wood;

o adulteration of the charcoal with stones, earth and dirt, a problem especially common with pit and mound kilns.

As the manufacture of charcoal is often thought to be an important cause of deforestation and land degradation, there is a clear need to improve the efficiency of biomass-to-charcoal conversion. The scope for technical improvements in the design and operation of pit and mound kilns is often considerable, including changes in fuel-stacking methods and the use of chimneys. Such modifications can increase yields by significant amounts, typically 30 per cent over the yields of traditional kilns, with extra capital costs often less than US$50 per kiln. However, some traditional kilns operate extremely efficiently.

With all charcoal production technologies, one of the most critical determinants of conversion efficiency is the care with which the kiln is operated. For example, wood must be dried and carefully stacked to provide an even flow of air through the kiln, allowing sufficient time for reactions to take place. Incorrect operation can easily reduce yields by 50 per cent, and

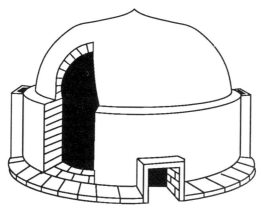

Figure 24 *The beehive brick kiln*

operators will need thorough training and technical support if they are to achieve high yields. Some technologies are more vulnerable than others to the inefficient practices described above and to high moisture content. Brick kilns have particular advantages in this respect; metal mound and pit kilns tend to be operated in the dry season only, although in some areas, such as southern Thailand, the wood is dried inside the kiln.

Two modern kiln designs are the portable metal kiln and the beehive brick kiln. The metal kiln is a cylinder with a conical top. It breaks down into two or three components which are rolled easily along the forest floor to new burn areas, or are transported by truck. It usually costs US$500 to $3000, with yields of 20 to 30 per cent. The beehive is a half-spherical brick kiln (Figure 24) which costs US$200 to $700 for small kilns of up to about 20 m³ with yields of up to 35 per cent. Larger kilns, of about 70 m³, can cost up to US$10000.

Both designs tend to be used by licensed charcoal dealers or forestry departments rather than by the small users in the informal sector who, unless assisted in both technique and marketing, cannot afford and/or benefit from improved kilns.

Problems and successes

There are two main problems in introducing improved charcoal technologies. The first is the difficulty of finding and training charcoal operators who can take advantage of new or improved technologies and training the extension workers needed for widespread application of improvements. The second is the limited extent to which any changes are acceptable or profitable to existing producers. As, in many countries, charcoal making is carried out in the informal sector, is usually seasonal, sometimes illegal, and often a source of income of the last resort, the prices received by producers are usually extremely low in relation to the retail prices obtained in urban areas; and transport and the margins of several stages of trading and marketing account for the difference. Around Addis Ababa, for example, retail prices can often be well over five times the price paid for the charcoal at the production site. In this context, the introduction of even simple low-cost changes to production techniques, or new low-cost kilns such as permanent mud beehives, can be extremely difficult to undertake, as the benefits may not be easily apparent.

In other instances, where charcoal is carried out on a large scale by highly organized groups operating in the informal sector, yields may be very high, so that few improvements are needed.

Fuelwood production activities closely linked with improvements in charcoal production will often be a necessary condition of success. Switching to larger, more capital-intensive technologies with better efficiency may be possible, but the economic and social implications for traditional producers, and the rural economy as a whole, are likely to be adverse, especially if adequate wood production is not planned for in conjunction with the establishment of the new plant.

Where new kilns, such as the portable metal kiln, are introduced in large numbers, a major problem is management. The Mahawelli project in Sri Lanka came to a halt because the management company was unable to ensure production costs low enough to meet those of competing fuels such as imported coal.

One of the few successful cases is Uganda, where portable metal kilns were introduced on a closely controlled basis, providing charcoal for the domestic market. Licences were provided, together with financial assistance and technical training, by and under the strict control of the forestry department. In Brazil and Argentina, there is wide-scale success with brick kilns supplying charcoal for industry. In both cases, the economic, social and institutional parameters determined the success of the projects rather than the technologies chosen; the large-scale commercial demand for charcoal allowed the emergence of a highly organized, self-sustaining charcoal industry.

BRIQUETTING

In many developing countries significant quantities of crop residues are not used for fuel or other purposes because their low density makes them expensive to transport, store, handle and combust. This problem can be overcome by compacting the residues through the application of pressure, and often heat as well, in piston, extrusion or other presses. This compresses the loose residues into a hard, high-density fuel (preferably 0.8 to 1.1 tonnes/m^3).

The term briquetting is often used to cover the three main methods of compacting: briquetting, cubing and pelletizing.

o   *Briquetting*   This technology uses screw or ram presses to extrude continuous logs through a die.

o   *Cubing*   This is the application of pressure to one or more moveable sides of a box containing the material.

o   *Pelletizing*   Pelletizing machinery uses a series of steel rolls to squeeze the material through a number of dies.

Because of the very high costs of pelletizing machinery and the relatively low quality of the product from cubing presses, these two processes will not be covered in this book.

Before briquetting, most biomass materials must be dried and reduced in size by chipping or crushing. Binders are used in some cases, usually starches or molasses, but they tend to be expensive. The smell of burning binders can also be offensive, particularly in household use. Other technical variations include carbonizing the material before briquetting, a technique which also requires a binder. A number of projects using this approach have been established in India and Nepal, although their success is questionable.

Cost effectiveness of briquetting

Mechanically powered briquetting machinery is manufactured mainly in the developed countries, with outputs ranging from 120 kg/h to 5 t/h, and costs of US$10000 to $100000 depending on the output and the type of raw material to be used. At present, there appears to be only one Third World manufacturer, in Thailand, who is marketing a lower cost machine at about US$5000. Smaller powered briquetting machines, and animal- and human-powered machines, are also available, with capacities as low as 10 kg/h.

There has been increasing interest in residue briquetting for the developing countries in the past ten years, but unfortunately, many projects fail. Residue costs tend to be higher than expected, because of collection expenses and the increasing use of residues for fuel or other purposes. With the exception of very small-scale manual operations, briquetting machinery is usually capital intensive, and requires inputs such as energy, management, maintenance, technical skills, spare parts and foreign exchange. Finally, high production costs restrict the market for briquettes, while their characteristics do not allow them to meet the needs of household or industrial users without significant investment in modifications to combustion equipment.

Future technical changes may simplify briquetting systems, reducing energy needs and costs. Under these circumstances, and especially if fuel costs rise significantly, the potential contribution of briquetting to more effective utilization of unused residues could be realized.

A wood-fired gasifier with diesel generating set

PRODUCER GAS

Producer gas is formed from the partial combustion of biomass in the presence of controlled amounts of air. It is a gas of low calorific value, formed mainly of carbon monoxide and hydrogen. It can be burned directly to provide process heat, or cooled and cleaned for use in internal combustion engines as a partial or complete substitute for liquid fossil fuels.

Producer gas used as a fuel directly for industrial heat processes is extremely attractive because, unlike raw biomass, it is clean, easy to control and its combustion is generally more efficient.

Producer gas is in relatively common use for the provision of heat for large-scale process systems in the industrialized world. There are significant plants in a few developing countries, especially Brazil, and in small- to medium-sized industries in south-east Asia, where their performance is well proven. However, their wider use in developing countries and at smaller scales is limited by the small amount of research undertaken on appropriate systems and the lack of field practice. There are signs that interest in producer gas for small heat systems is increasing, and there should be wider field experience on a small scale within the next few years.

BIOGAS AS A FUEL

Biogas is produced naturally by the action of certain bacteria on water-logged organic materials in the absence of air: a process known as 'anaerobic digestion'. It consists of about 60 per cent methane while the

84

remaining 40 per cent is mainly inert carbon dioxide. As a fuel, raw biogas has a calorific value of about 23MJ/m³. The carbon dioxide can be removed by bubbling the raw biogas through slaked lime (calcium hydroxide), but this process requires regular replacement of the lime. After this treatment, known as 'scrubbing', biogas approximates to pure methane with a calorific value of about 40 MJ/m³.

The main uses of biogas are cooking, heating water and lighting (with gas lamps using incandescent mantles). It is also an attractive fuel for use with internal combustion engines since it is relatively free of pollutants that can cause damage. Biogas has excellent anti-knock properties and can be safely used as the sole fuel with very high compression ratio spark-ignition engines. It can also be used with unmodified diesel engines, but only as a supplementary fuel because diesel is needed to fire the mixture; this can generally reduce diesel requirements by 50 to 70 per cent. Some special biogas engines have been built, which run on 100 per cent biogas more efficiently than an unconverted petrol engine.

Biogas digester designs

Recent efforts have been made to popularize the use of biogas in Asia, mainly in China, but also in India, Nepal and some of the south-east Asian countries. Commercial biogas units have also gone into production in various countries, including the USA, UK, Australia and Kenya, as well as in China and India (the two countries making the most use of the technology). The two main types of small-scale biogas digester were originally devloped in China and India.

Chinese biogas digester
The Chinese biogas digester is situated entirely underground (Figure 25)

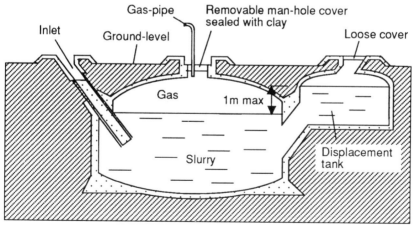

Figure 25 *The Chinese biogas digester*

Construction of a family biogas digester in China

and consists of a concrete-lined pit with a concrete dome. It is completely filled with slurry, and gas, as it begins to form, collects under the dome and forces down the level of the slurry by up to 1 m. The gas pressure is consequently variable depending on the volume of gas stored, but by using a simple manometer on the gas line it is possible to gain an accurate indication of the amount of gas available.

Indian biogas digester
This is more expensive to construct because it has a steel gas holder; on the other hand it is less likely to leak than the Chinese design which requires extremely high quality internal plastering to avoid minute gas leaks. With the Indian design (Figure 26), gas collects under the steel gas-holder, which rises as it fills with gas. The slurry is simply contained in a brick-lined pit. The height of the gas holder out of the pit indicates the amount of gas available, and the pressure is determined by the weight and cross-sectional area of the gas holder.

Other types of digester range from large concrete chambers used in sewage works to single oil drums which can be adapted to make workable mini-digesters. The Chinese and Indian digesters illustrated are known as

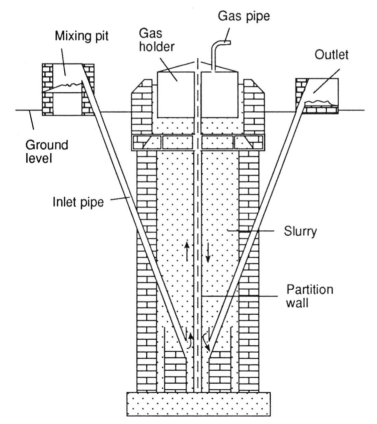

Figure 26 *The Indian biogas digester*

'continuous' digesters since they function with a regular throughput of material. An alternative approach used in some areas is the 'batch digester' where a quantity of material is sealed in a container for a period until it gases; once the process is complete the container is opened, emptied and refilled with fresh slurry. It is normal to have several batch digesters – usually at least three – working in cycles which are out of phase so that at least one unit is producing gas at any time.

Principal operating parameters

The biogas process requires an input material provided as a liquid slurry with around 5 to 10 per cent solids. It is important to use materials which break down readily: highly fibrous biomass such as wood or straw is not easily attacked and broken down by the bacteria, but softer feedstocks like dung and leaves react well to the process.

Internal temperature
For optimum performance, the internal temperature of a typical continuous biogas digester should be in the mid-30s°C; moreover, temperature conditions need to be as steady as possible. The digestion process generates a small amount of heat which helps to maintain the temperature, but in cooler climates or seasons the unit should be well insulated and may need heating during cold spells.

Retention time
The average retention time for the throughput of material for the complete process is normally 20 to 40 days. The actual digester size has to be equal to the design retention time in days, multiplied by the daily input rate: thus, with a 30-day retention time and 1 m^3/day of input, the digester volume would need to be 30 m^3. The longer the retention time and the warmer the digester, the more complete the process and the more energy per kilogram of volatile solids is obtained; however, the digester needs to be larger and more expensive. Hence the size and retention time are usually a compromise between keeping costs at a reasonable level and obtaining complete digestion.

Loading rate and moisture content
The loading rate and the moisture content are related; the slurry needs to be kept to around 85 to 95 per cent liquid. Too thin a slurry takes up more volume and requires a bigger digester than necessary, while too thick a slurry limits mixing and tends to solidify and clog the unit.

Carbon/nitrogen ratio
Another important criterion is the carbon/nitrogen ratio: for efficient digestion the process requires between 20 and 30 parts of carbon per part of nitrogen. Certain carbon-rich materials like leaves or grass need to be mixed with nitrogen-rich substances such as urine or poultry droppings. Alternatively, ammonia or other nitrogen-rich artificial chemicals may be added to a digester running mainly on vegetation.

Ouput

The output to be expected will be in the order of 0.1 to 0.7 m³/kg of volatile solids input per day.

Because biogas digesters are capable of storing about 12 hours supply of gas, an engine can be used that draws gas at quite a high rate. The size of engine is not critical since it is only the number of hours it will run that is governed by the digester's gas capacity.

Cost effectiveness

If biogas is used for domestic purposes, quite modest quantities are sufficient. For example, gas-rings used for cooking tend to need 250 to 500 litres of biogas per hour. Therefore, a typical family using two gas-rings for around a total of 2 h/day will consume about 1 to 2 m³ of biogas per day, a demand which can be readily met from two to three domestic animals plus household wastes and human excreta. Gas lights with mantles require around 100 to 120 litres of biogas per hour.

Significant inputs of waste material are required to yield even modest amounts of engine power. A small engine for irrigation pumping, with an output of one kW (hydraulic), will require about 256 m³ of biogas per day for four hours of daily operation. This amounts to some 370 to 2560 kg of input material per day. Therefore, in energy terms alone, the economics tend to be marginal in comparison with petroleum fuels. However, when the fertilizer value of the slurry (about 200 kg/day in the example, as the input solids are reduced to around 30 per cent in the output), plus the waste disposal benefits are considered, the process frequently comes out as an economically attractive option.

There is no doubt that the biogas process becomes significantly more cost effective in larger sizes. A survey of biogas units in India found a payback period of 23 years for a 2 m³ plant which dropped to three years with 10 m³ unit. The sizes of plant needed to run small engines are much bigger than this and are therefore likely to be more cost effective.

Heat conversion

STOVES

Most rural and low-income urban groups in developing countries use wood, charcoal or residues, or a combination of these, as their main source of fuel for cooking and heating. The stoves vary widely, but in general urban users cook on ceramic or ceramic and metal stoves manufactured by local potters and metal artisans, while other urban groups and rural people use open fires or simple ceramic or mud-shielded fires. Most mud stoves are made by the users themselves, while other stoves are usually produced by local potters.

A Kenya jiko stove in use

An ITDG improved stove in Sri Lanka

For the past fifteen years there have been many national and international programmes to introduce more efficient biomass stoves into households in both rural and urban areas. The main original objective was fuel savings (figures as high as 50 per cent were often quoted), both to reduce deforestation and to help low-income families reduce their expenditure on fuels. However, the lack of any large-scale success has prompted a revaluation of these objectives in recent years. The causal links between household fuel consumption and deforestation have been found to be less convincing in many instances; reductions in fuel consumption, often much less than predicted in laboratory trials, are not necessarily as highly rated among users as previously thought.

It is now clear that better stoves can make a valuable contribution to kitchen management and the quality of household life, but often because of smoke reduction, and faster and safer cooking. Reduced fuel consumption may accompany these benefits, but it is not necessarily, in the eyes of the user, the main reason for which a new stove is purchased.

Stoves programmes

Recent stoves programmes have tended to focus on the alleviation of the dependency of poor households on biomass and on improvements in their quality of life. As women are nearly always the users of household stoves, these programmes have established close links with programmes addressing issues of particular interest to women. Stoves programmes are also moving into small institutional and commercial stoves, sometimes at the household level. Environmental protection and reduced vulnerability to disasters remain a long-term aim, especially since fuel shortages are expected to become more severe. Sustainable production of stoves and better quality and more rewarding jobs are also important objectives.

Methodologies for the development and implementation of stoves programmes are now well developed for a wide range of stoves. Fuels include wood, charcoal, briquettes and crop and animal residues; the stoves may be a single-pot or double-pot and with or without a chimney. The methodologies include needs assessment, stove design, testing and evaluation, pilot projects, commercial manufacture and dissemination.

Designs and performance

Stove designs are not static: recent research has shown that many different stove designs have been developed over very long periods of time to meet the changing cooking requirements of different ethnic and social groups. Stoves originally evolved in one society have been introduced to others, and local modifications have often been carried out to suit local practices and needs, as in the case of the Kenya jiko (Figure 27).

Figure 27 *The Kenya jiko stove*

The performance of new stoves usually depends on some or all of the following requirements being met:

○ consistent manufacturing quality;

○ correct installation;

○ proper maintenance;

○ continuous adaptation of designs and manufacturing methods to meet new and changing user needs;

○ continuous monitoring of programmes to ensure that the above requirements are met.

Most of the problems now encountered in the implementation of stoves programmes increasingly relate to the difficulties of meeting these requirements, rather than the design of the stoves themselves.

INDUSTRIAL COMBUSTION

Wood and agricultural residues are the main fuels used for industrial processing in rural areas and many urban areas of developing countries. The use of biomass fuels can be a major cause of both localized and more widespread deforestation, and as biomass fuels become scarce and prices increase, the viability of rural industries is often undermined. There are thus both economic and environmental grounds for improving the efficiency of industrial biomass combustion systems.

The range of industries using biomass fuels is extremely wide, including tea, rubber, coconut, bricks, lime, baking, tobacco, sugar and many other food and agricultural product processing industries; institutions include restaurants, hospitals, schools, prisons, barracks and hotels.

Improving efficiency

Although the combustion devices used by these industries are as varied as the industries themselves, a common feature is inefficiency. The devices are often simple brick structures with very crude grates, and there is little knowledge of complete combustion or of the advantages of matching heat exchangers to furnaces and stoves. Despite the vast amount of work that has been carried out on wood gasification for power, there has been little recognition of its scope for heat, where it can make significant improvements in efficiency, and also of product quality. In contrast, recent years have seen a very high level of research on these issues in the developed world; analytical and design methodologies have been developed and commercial units are available. But little of this new approach has been adapted to the needs of rural industries in developing countries to provide low-cost, efficient, easily operated furnaces and kilns.

For these rural industries the cost of fuel is a measurable and often significant component of production or running costs, so that the benefits of fuel reductions can translate into immediate cost savings. The successful improvement of combustion systems can be found in a range of industries: in the Kenyan tobacco industry, for example, changes in kiln design and operation have reduced wood consumption from as much as 16 kg per kilogram of dried tobacco to as little as 5 kg.

Methodologies

Methodologies for the design and development of more efficient combustion systems are well known in some areas. Unfortunately, methods which address needs assessment, matching designs to actual technical and financial needs and resources, and evaluation and dissemination, are not as well developed. Unlike stoves programmes, where energy costs are now viewed in the overall context of kitchen management and houshold requirements, the evaluation of the energy needs of rural industry in terms of its overall development is still rare, except in major export or plantation industries such as tea or sugar.

An example of the importance of this approach can be seen in the Thai brick industry, where an examination of energy needs shows that major fuel savings can be made. However, the investments needed can only take place with a change in product range to allow the industry to compete successfully with the products of the cement industry.

An important constraint on the successful development of effective programmes is the poor provision and quality of data on the industrial use of woodfuels. This applies both to fuel consumption patterns and information on existing technologies. Most fuel consumption figures are crudely estimated, with little or no reference to fuel sources or prices. Similarly, there is little published data on the very few attempts to introduce improved

93

furnaces. The reports that have appeared suggest that success is rare: capital costs of improved furnaces have been too high, training has been inadequate and field results have been inferior to laboratory tests.

Power for conversion

PRODUCER GAS FOR POWER

The advantage of producer gas over other biomass-fuelled power systems is that, at least in theory, existing diesel engines can be converted to dual fuel operation using producer gas with 15 to 20 per cent diesel fuel gas, merely by retro-fitting low-cost gas generators. This requires only minor modifications, thus minimizing capital costs.

Although there are many different designs, most gasifiers are of the downdraught type (Figure 28), in which air is drawn through the burning bed. Conversion efficiencies (energy in the gas/energy in the fuel) of 70 per cent are common.

For use in engines, producer gas is cleaned and cooled in a wide range of scrubbers, filters, electrostatic precipitators and other machinery. The gas can then be mixed with diesel to power a diesel engine, or used alone to fuel a petrol engine. The calorific value of the gas is approximately one

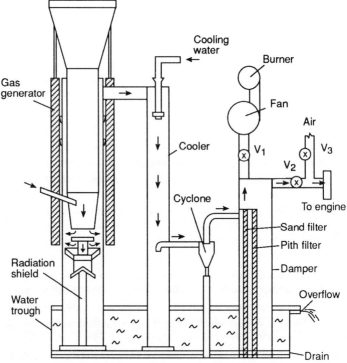

Figure 28 *A producer gasifier of the downdraught type*

third that of petroleum fuels, and engines have to be derated when run on producer gas.

Performance

Several hundred small – up to 50 kW – producer gas power systems have been established in developing countries, but their performance is a controversial issue. There have been many claims of success, but the evidence for long-term commercial operation on a smaller scale is not yet convincing.

The main problem in the technical areas is that the gas given off from most fuels contains a high proportion of tarry substances and small particles which, if not removed, can dramatically reduce the lifetime of modern high-speed diesels. Cleaning the gas sufficiently to give the ease of operation and long life normally expected from diesel engines is technically possible but expensive, especially on a small scale in isolated rural areas. Where less effective cleaning is carried out, the wear on the engine increases rapidly due to entrainment of particulate matter in the gas stream. Poor filter design and maintenance can also contribute to this problem. Finally, field operations have not achieved the efficiencies obtained from laboratory tests, and fuel consumption is often higher than expected.

The choice of fuel and fuel processing is another important factor. Charcoal is the preferred fuel because gas cleaning is much easier than with raw biomass, but the overall efficiency (raw biomass to shaft power) is very low (< 10 per cent) because of low raw-biomass-to-charcoal conversion efficiencies. However, using raw biomass presents further technical and financial problems in sizing, ensuring the correct moisture content, and extra gas cleaning.

Viability

In this context, it is difficult to draw conclusions about the viability of producer gas for shaft power, but the following is probably acceptable to most parties involved in the producer gas industry. At output levels of 25 to 50 kW, producer gas systems do not appear to be commercially proven, although they are technically viable for charcoal, the fuel to which they are best suited, and to a certain extent for wood chips.

At lower outputs, below 10 kW, the long-term technical viability of even charcoal-fuelled systems in the field is still in doubt, although in Thailand, where charcoal is very cheap, the Asian Institute of Technology suggests that small systems are financially viable. Above the 25 to 50 kW level, charcoal-fuelled systems appear to be commercially viable in some cases, as do systems fuelled with wood chips. However, even at this level, agricultural residues have not been proven as fuels.

The doubts about producer gas power systems indicate that considerable development work is still required on the design and operation of reliable,

A 3hp steam engine at the Centre for Alternative Technology, Wales

low maintenance and low-cost gas cleaning systems, especially for fuels other than charcoal.

STEAM ENGINES

Steam engines fuelled by coal or biomass were the traditional source of power for much industrial processing and large-scale agriculture before modern energy systems came into existence. Even now, steam engines of 80 to 400 kW are still in use in sawmills and sugar, rice and furniture mills in several parts of the world, while manufacturers of medium-to-large steam engines still exist in Thailand and Latin America. However, most steam plant is over 40 years old: much is now being replaced by grid systems, turbines or diesel because of the high costs of spare parts.

Steam is raised in a boiler heated by a furnace, usually fuelled by wood or agricultural residues from a mill, then passed into the engine. The exhaust steam may be passed through a condenser to recover heat for drying, boiling or preserving, for example, while the water obtained can be recycled as feed-water to the boiler. Efficiencies are 4 to 15 per cent for power applications and up to 50 per cent in combined heat and power mode.

Small steam systems have a number of advantages over producer gas plant: they are more reliable, they can supply steam direct for process heat, and they are fuel flexible. However, capital costs are extremely high and the need for a boiler puts the plant within safety legislation in most countries,

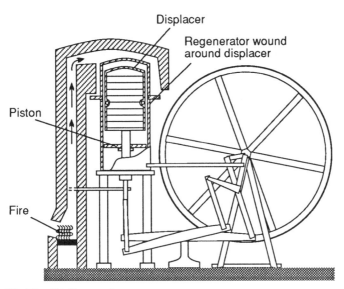

Figure 29 *The Stirling engine*

which requires the formal training of operators and annual insurance inspection and tests, adding to costs and causing extra problems for management.

There are no suppliers of steam plant in the 20 to 100 kW range that meet the techncial and financial needs of industry and the energy sectors of developing countries. However, companies in the UK, Australia and the US are now developing small steam systems which may yet meet these needs.

STIRLING ENGINES

In the Stirling engine, the products of combustion pass around a cylinder, heating a charge gas enclosed within the cylinder by a piston (Figure 29). As the gas temperature increases, so it expands, driving a piston; a cycle of heating, cooling and reheating provides the continuous drive needed. The Stirling engine is completely fuel flexible, and is theoretically more efficient than internal combustion and steam engines. Unlike other systems, it does not need a boiler. Thus in many respects, it is the ideal biomass-fuelled power system.

The development of very sophisticated Stirling engines using helium or hydrogen charge gases at extremely high pressures is proceeding rapidly in the industrialized world. However, at present only one low-pressure air-charged Stirling engine is available which comes close to meeting the needs of developing countries: this is the 5 kW Hamara engine, made in India. Over 100 of these engines are in operation in the field, powering rice mills fuelled with rice husks. However, under present circumstances the Stirling engine does not compare competitively with diesel plant.

97

Annexe I   Further information

CHAPTER 2 POWER FROM SOLAR ENERGY

References and bibliography

Derrick, A., Francis, C. and Bokalders, V., *Solar Photovoltaic Products: A Guide for Development Workers*, IT Publications, London, 1989.

Dorrenbos, J., and Pruitt, W.O., *Crop-water requirements*, FAO, Rome, 1977.

Kenna, J. and Gillett, B., *Solar Water Pumping: A Handbook*, IT Publications, London, 1985.

McNelis, B., Derrick, A. and Starr, M., *Solar-powered Electricity: A Survey of Photovoltaic Power in Developing Countries*, IT Publications, London, 1988.

Rentch, U.R.S., *Solar Photovoltaics for Irrigation Water Pumping*, SKAT, St Gallen, 1982.

Solar energy organizations

International Solar Energy Society, PO Box 52, Parkville Vic 3052 Australia.

The UK Solar Energy Society, King's College London. Atkins Building South (128), Campden Hill Road, London W8 7AH, UK.

Solar Energy Unit, University College of Wales, Newport Road, Cardiff CF2 1TA, UK.

CHAPTER 3 HEAT FROM SOLAR ENERGY

References and bibliography

Action/Peace Corps and VITA, *Preparing Grain for Storage*, Action/Peace Corps and VITA, Arlington, 1976.

Brace Research Institute, *A Survey of Solar Agricultural Driers*, Brace Research Institute, Quebec, 1975.

Brace Research Institute, *How to Build a Solar Water Heater*, Brace Research Institute, Quebec, 1979.

Brinkworth, B.J., *Solar Energy for Man*, Crompton Press, London, 1972.

Commonwealth Science Council, *Solar Driers*, Commonwealth Science Council, London, 1985.

Deuss, Bart, *The Zig Zag Collector*, TOOL, Amsterdam, 1987.

ILO, *Solar Drying: Practical Methods of Food Preservation*, ILO, Geneva 1986.

Malik, A.S. et al., *Solar Distillation*, Pergamon Press, UK, 1982.

McCarthy, K., and Ford, B., *Practical Solar Heating*, Prism Press, Dorset, 1978.

Plante, R.H., *Solar Domestic Hot Water*, Wiley, UK, 1983.

UK-ISES, *Heating Water by the Sun*, Intern. Solar Energy Soc., U.K., 1981.

Solar Energy Organizations

See references for Chapter 2.

CHAPTER 4 POWER FROM THE WIND

References and bibliography

Golding, E.W., *The Generation of Electricity by Wind Power*, SPON, Trowbridge, 1976.

Lancashire, S.J., et al., *Windpump Handbook*, IT Publications, London, 1987.

Lysen, E.H., *Introduction to Wind Energy*, SWD, The Netherlands, 1982.

Mann, R.D., *How to Build a 'Cretan Sail' Windpump*, IT Publications, London, 1979.

McGuigan, Dermot, *Small Scale Wind Power*, Prism Press, Dorset, 1978.

Park, Jack, *The Wind Power Book*, Cheshire Books, USA, 1981.

Wind energy organizations

British Wind Energy Association, 4 Hamilton Place, London W1V OBQ, UK.

CHAPTER 5 WATER POWER

References and bibliography

Hamm, H.W., *Low-cost Development of Small Water Power Sites*, VITA, Virginia, 1989.

Hangzhou Regional Centre for Small Hydro Power, *Small Hydro Power in China*, IT Publications, London, 1985.

Hislop, D., *Upgrading Micro-hydro in Sri Lanka*, IT Publications, London, 1986.

Hofkes, E.H. and Visscher, J.T., *Renewable Energy Sources for Rural Water Supply in Developing Countries*, International Reference Centre for Community Water Supply and Sanitation, The Hague, 1986.

Holland, R., *Micro-hydro Electric Power*, IT Publications, London, 1983.

Inversin, Allen R., *Micro-hydropower Sourcebook: A Practical Guide to Design and Implementation in Developing Countries*, NRECA, New York, 1986.

Iversen, H.W., 'An Analysis of the Hydraulic Ram', *Journal of Fluids Engineering*, Transactions of the American Society of Mechanical Engineers, 1985.

Kindel, E.W., *A Hydraulic Ram for Village Use* VITA, USA, 1970 and 1975.

Meier, Ueli, *Local Experience with a Micro-hydro Technology*, SKAT, St Gallen, 1981.

Watt, S.B., *A Manual on the Hydraulic Ram for Pumping Water*, IT Publications, London, 1975.

Crossflow Turbine Fabrication Manual, Vols 1–8, SKAT, St Gallen, 1990.

Water power organizations

Centre for Alternative Technology, Machynlleth, Powys, Wales SY20 9AZ, UK.

Intermediate Technology Development Group, Myson House, Railway Terrace, Rugby, Warwickshire CV21 3HT, UK.

Local Water Authority (see under 'Water' in telephone directory).

National Association of Water Power Users, The Rock, South Brent, Devon TQ10 9JL, UK.

CHAPTER 6 BIOMASS

References and bibliography

Approvecho Institute, *Small-scale Production and Use (of Charcoal)*, GATE/Vieweg, Braunschweig, 1984.

Arends, G., and Dekersloot-Shoug, S., *An Overview of Possible Uses of Sawdust*, TOOL, Amsterdam, 1985.

Barnard, G., and Foley, G., 'Biomass Gasification in Developing Countries', *Earthscan Energy Information Programme Technical Report No. 1*, IIED, London, 1983.

Caceres, R., et al. (eds.), *Stoves for People*, IT Publications, London, 1989.

Clarke, Robin, (ed.), *Woodstoves Dissemination*, IT Publications, London, 1985.

Eriksson, S., and Prior, M., *The Briquetting of Agricultural Wastes for Fuel*, FAO Environment and Energy Paper, Rome, 1990.

FAO, *The Use of Wood Fuels in Rural Industries in Asia and the Pacific Region*, FAO Regional Wood Development Programme, Bangkok, 1988.

FAO, *Stoves Programmes in Asia – A Status Report*, FAO Regional Wood Development Programme, Bangkok, 1988.

Foley, Gerald, 'Charcoal-making in Developing Countries', *Earthscan Energy Information Programme Technical Report No. 5*, IIED, London, 1986.

Fulford, D., *Running a Biogas Programme*, IT Publications, London, 1988.

Joseph, S., *The Stove Project Manual: Planning and Implementation*, IT Publications, London, 1985.

Meynell, P.J., *Methane: Planning a Digester*, Prism Press, Dorset, 1982.

Micuta, W., *Modern Stoves for All*, IT Publications/Bellerive, London, 1986.

National Research Council, *Another Fuel for Motor Transport (Producer Gas)* National Academy Press, Washington DC, 1983.

National Resources Institute, *A Profile of the Briquetting of Agricultural and Forestry Residues (Ref. G. 181)*, 1983.

Sasse, Ludwig, *Biogas Plants*, GATE Vieweg & Sohn, Braunschweig, 1988.

Stewart, W., et al., *Improved Wood, Waste and Charcoal Burning Stoves: A Practitioner's Manual*, IT Publications, London, 1987.

Van Buren, A., *A Chinese Biogas Manual*, IT Publications, London, 1979.

Annexe II   Equipment suppliers and manufacturers

Please note that this is a selective list and does not imply endorsement.

SOLAR ENERGY

The companies listed below are the major suppliers and manufacturers of solar electrical equipment and collectors for solar water heaters. The market is rapidly changing, however, and new companies are continually entering the market.

PV module suppliers

AEG TELEFUNKEN, Industriestrasse 29, D-200, Wedel, Holstein, Germany

ARCO SOLAR, PO Box 6032, Camarillo, CA 93010, USA

BP SOLAR SYSTEMS, Aylesbury Vale Industrial Park, Stocklake, Aylesbury, Bucks HP20 1DQ, UK

BHEL, PV Division, Vikasnagar, Mysore Road, Bangalore 560 025, India

CENTRAL ELECTRONICS LIMITED, 4 Industrial Area, Sahibabad 201 010, UP, India

HELIODINAMICA, Caixa Postal 8085, 9051, Sao Paulo-SP, Brazil

HOXAN, 13–12 Ginza, 5 Chome Chuo Ku, Tokyo 104, Japan

ISOFOTON SA, Oficina Central, cul Miguel Angel, 16, 28010 Madrid, Spain

INSTERSOLAR LIMITED, Factory 3, Cock Lane, High Wycombe, Bucks, UK

ITALSOLAR, Via A D'Andrea 6, 00048, Nettuno (RM), Italy

KYOCERA, Chiba Sakura, –3 Ohsaku 1-Chome Sakura-Shi, Chiba Pref. 285, Japan

PHOTOWATT INTERNATIONAL SA, 131 Route de l'Empereur, 92500 Rueil-Malmaison, France

R & S RENEWABLE ENERGY SYSTEMS, P O Box 45, 5600 AA Eindhoven, The Netherlands

SHOWA ARCO SOLAR, 10 Anson Road 18–24, International Plaza, Singapore 0207

SIEMENS SOLAR GMBH, Buchenallee 3, D-5060, Bergisch Gladbach, Germany

SOLAREX CORPORATION, 1335 Piccard Drive, P O Box 6008, Rockville, Maryland 20850, USA

SOVONICS, 1100 West Maple Road, Troy, Michigan 48084, USA

Suppliers of PV pumps

AEG Industriaestrasse 29, D-200 Wedel, Holstein, Germany

BP SOLAR SYSTEMS, Aylesbury Vale Industrial Park, Stockdale, Aylesbury, Bucks HP20 1DQ, UK

ERGO INDUSTRISE (CANADA) INC, 201–1777 W, 8th Avenue, Vancouver, BC V6J 1V8, Canada

AY MACDONALD MANUFACTURING COMPANY, 4800 Chavenelle Road, Dubuque, IA 5200, USA

GRUNDFOS INTERNATIONAL A/S, DK-8850, Bjerroingbo, Denmark

ITALSOLAR, Via A D'Andrea 6, 00048 Nettuno (RM), Italy

MONO PUMPS LIMITED, Cromwell Road Trading Estate, Cromwell Road, Bredbury, Stockport, SK6 2RF, UK

SIEMENS SOALR GMBH, Buchenallee 3, D-5060, Bergisch Gladbach, Germany

SOLAR ELECTRIC INTERNTIONAL, 77 Luqua Industrial Estate, Luqua, Malta

TOTAL ENERGIE, 24 rue Joannes Masse, 69009 Lyon, France

Suppliers of PV refrigerators

The World Health Organisation (WHO), in its EPI Technical Series publishes a document entitled *The Cold Chain Product Information Sheets.* This catalogues equipment which has undergone tests to verify that performance is of a standard acceptable to WHO and United Nations Children Fund (UNICEF). The document may be obtained from The Cold Chain Unit, Expanded Programme on Immunization, WHO Health Organisation, 1211 Geneva 27, Switzerland.

Lighting system suppliers

AEG, Industriaestrasse 29, D-2000 Wedel, Holstein, Germany

BP SOLAR SYSTEMS, Aylesbury Vale Industrial Park, Stocklake, Aylesbury, Bucks, HP20 1DQ, UK

FNMA, 14 rue Limete, BP 1967, Kinshasa 1, Zaire

ITALSOLAR, Via A D'Andrea 6, 00048 Nettuno (RM), Italy

LEROY SOMER, vi of Agriers, 16015 Angouleme, France

NOACK SOLAR, Kjelsaaveien 160, Box 79, Kjelsaas, Oslo 4, Norway

POLAR PRODUCTS, 2808 Oregon Courst, Building 4, Torrance CA, USA

RENEWABLE ENERGY SYSTEMS BV, P O Box 45, 5600 Eindhoven, The Netherlands

SOLAREX, 1335 Piccard Drive, P O Box 6008, Rockville, MD 20850, USA

SOLAR ENERGIE TECHNIK, Postfach 1180, Altlussheim, Germany.

WIND POWER

Windpump suppliers and manufacturers

ABACHEM LIMITED, Newark, Nottinghamshire, UK

AEROMOTOR, P O Box 1364, Conway, Arkansas, 72032, USA

ALSTON WINDMILLS LIMITED, Branthorne Street, Gisborne, Victoria, Australia

AMIHAN UTATA, Wat Hydroelectric Systems Inc, 304 J Rizal Street, Mandaluyong, MM, Philippines 792717

BHARAT HEAVY ELECTRICAL LIMITED, Corporate R & D Division, Vikas Nagar, Hyderabad 500 593, India

CAVENTO, Empresa Brasileira de Equipamentos Industriais & Agricolas Limited, Ce 021 KM06 Maranguape 10 Distrito Industrial do Ceara, Brazil, Sidney Williams & Company (Pty) Limited, P O Box 22.

COMET, Bulwich Hill, NSW 2203, Australia

HAYES (NZ) LIMITED, P O Box 23-042, Christchurch 4, New Zealand

KIJITO, Bobs Harries Engineering Limited, P O Box 40, Karamani Estate, Thika, Kenya

MERIN LIMITED, P O Box 4145, Karachi 2, Pakistan

METALURGIA BELGRANO 728, Piso 1, Buenos Aires, Argentina

RAYMILL STEEL PRODUCTS LIMITED, Sta. Rose, Nueva Ecija, Philippines

SOUTHERN CROSS, Toowoomba Foundry Pty Limited, 259 Ruthven, Toowoomba, Australia 4350

THAI U. SA INDUSTRIAL FACTORY, No. 5g/15 M007, 2 Pracharaj, 2 Road, Dusit, Bangkok, Thailand

TRYLON WINDPUMP, The Wind Turbine Company of Canada, 21 Howard Avenue, Elmira, Ontario N3B 2C9, Canada

STEWART & LLOYDS, Bulawayo, Zimbabwe

WIND ENERGY UNIT, Water Resources Board, 2A Gregory's Avenue, Colombo 7, Sri Lanka

WIND BARON, Wind Baron Corporation, 3702 West Lower Buckeye Road, Phoenix, Arizona 85009, USA.

Windpumps are also manufactured in Colombia, Finland, the People's Republic of China and the Soviet Union.

Wind generators manufacturers and suppliers

There are many wind generator manufacturers in the USA, Europe and Japan but, with the exception of Argentina, the People's Republic of China and India, there are few wind generator manufacturers in developing countries.

ALTERNATIVES, 37 Bangalla Street, Toowong, Brisbane, Q 4066, Australia

AERODYN, Redderbek 1, d-2333 Damendorf, Germany

AEROPOWER SYSTEMS, 2398 Forth St., Berkeley, CA 94701, USA

AIOLOS, Einsteinstraat 8a, 8606 JR Sneek, The Netherlands

BERGEY WINDPOWER COMPANY, 2000 Priestly Av., Norman, OK 73069, USA

BONUS ENERGY, Fabriksvej 4, DK-7330 Brande, Denmark

CATAVENOS, Rua Joao Sana, 66-C Postal, Encantado, RS, Brazil

CHALK WIND SYSTEMS, PO Box 446 St Cloud, PLA 32769, USA

DANSIK VINDKRAFT IND., Vedevej 6, Bureso, Denmark 335550

DUNLITE, PO Box 100, Hindermarsh, Adelaide, SA 5007, Australia

DYNERGY CORP, 12269 Uno Avenue Laconia NH 03246, USA

ELEXTRO GMBH, St Gallerstrasse 27 8400 Winterthur, Switzerland

ENAG S.A. Route de Pont l'Abbe, 29000, Quimper, France

ENERGY SYSTEMS INTERNATIONAL, PO Box E444, Cabera ACT 260, Australia

HMZ, Rellestraat 3, 3800 Sint Truiden, Belgium

KEDCO INC, 9016, Aviation Boulevard, Inglewood, CA 90301, USA

LUBING WINDKRAFTECNIK GMBH, Friesenstrasse 1, D-2840, Diepholz 1 postfach 50, 06, 8000 Munchen 50, Germany

MARLEC, Unit K, Cavendish Rd, Corby, Northants, NN17 1DZ, UK

NOAH ENERGY SYSTEMS GMBH, Michlenstrasse 11, D-53, Bonn, Germany

NORDTANK, 8 Nyballevej, DK 8444 Balle, Denmark

NORTH WIND POWER COMPANY, Box 315 Warren, VT 05674, USA

PI SPECIALIST ENGINEERS LTD, The Dean, Alresford, Hampshire, UK

RIVA CALZONI, Via Emilia Ponente 72, 40133, Bologna, Italy

SUDWIND, Kopenicker Strasse 145, D-1000, Berlin, Germany

VESTAS, Smed Hansens Vej, 6940, Lem, Denmark

WHIRLWIND POWER COMPANY, 5030 York Street, Denver, CO 80216, USA

WIND ENERGY COMPANY, 77 Drover Road, Rose Bay, Syndey, 2029 NSW, Australia

WEG, 345 Ruislip Road, Southall, Middlesex, UB1 2QX, UK

WINDSOL, 18 Chatzopoulou St, 176 71, Kallithea, Greece.

MICRO-HYDRO MANUFACTURERS, AGENTS AND CONSULTANTS

AVON ENGINEERING, PO Box 608, Ringwood, Hants BH24 1YE, UK

AVR HYDROPOWER LIMTED, Telford Building, Meadow Road, Salford M7 9PN, UK

BALAJU YANTRA SHALA (P) LIMITED, PO Box 209, Kathmandu, Nepal

BAMFORD, Whitehill Street West, Stockport, Cheshire SK4 1NT, UK

BROWN AND COMPANY, 48 Darley Road, Colombo, Sri Lanka

BUTWAL ENGINEERING WORKS (PVT) LIMITED, PO Box 1, Butwal, Nepal

DULAS ENGINEERING LTD, The Old School, Eglwysfach, Machynlleth, Powys, Wales SY20 8SX

EVANS ENGINEERING, Trecarrell Mill, Trebullet, Launceston, Cornwall, UK

GILBERT GILKES AND GORDON, Kendal, Cumbria LA9 7BZ, UK

G.P. ELECTRONICS, Pottery Road, Bovey Tracey, Devon, UK

P.C. HETTIARATCHI SYSTEM ENGINEERING, 131 Anderson Road, Dehiwala, Sri Lanka

KATHMANDU METAL INDUSTRY, Cha 3-812 Nagal Quadon, Kathmandu-3, Nepal

MACKELLAR, Strathspey Industrial Site, Granton-on-Spey, Morayshire PH26, UK

NEPAL YANTRA SHALA, Petan Industrial Estate, Petan, Nepal

TAMAR DESIGN PTY LIMITED, Deviot, Tasmania

WATER POWER ENGINEERING, Coaley Mill, Coaley, Gloucestershire GL11 5DS, UK

WEIR PUMPS, Newlands Road, Cathcart, Glasgow G44 4EX, UK

BIOMASS

Some of the technologies listed in this brief are site specific and/or one-offs, or are still under development. However the following sources of information are worth pursuing.

Combustion Systems

BIOMASS ENERGY SERVICES AND TECHNOLOGY, 5 Kenneth Avenue, Saratoga 2250, NSW, Australia

INTERMEDIATE TECHNOLOGY DEVELOPMENT GROUP, Myson House, Railway Terrace, Rugby CV21 3HT, UK

Producer Gas for Power

INDIAN INSTITUTE OF TECHNOLOGY, New Delhi, India

ASIAN INSTITUTE OF TECHNOLOGY, Bangkok, Thailand

Producer Gas for Heat

BIOMASS ENERGY SERVICES AND TECHNOLOGY, 5 Kenneth Avenue, Saratoga 2250, NSW, Australia

VENTEC (ENVIRONMENT) LTD., Lamarsh, Bures, Suffolk CO8 5EP, UK

Steam

AUSTRALIAN NATIONAL UNIVERSITY, Anutech Pty Ltd, GPO Box 4, Canberra ACT 2501, Australia

BIOMASS ENERGY SERVICES AND TECHNOLOGY, 5 Kenneth Avenue, Saratoga 2250, NSW, Australia

ENERGY FOR SUSTAINABLE DEVELOPMENT LTD., 51 Artesian Road, London W2 5DB, UK

FEZER SA, Steam Engines Division, Industrias Mecanicas, Cacador City, Santa Catalina, Brazil

MERNAK SA, Steam Engines Division, Industria Brasiliera de Maquinas, Cachoeir do Sul City, Riogrande do Sul, Brazil

SKINNER ENGINE COMPANY, Power Division, PO Box 1149, Erie, PA 16512, USA

SPILLINGWERK GMBH, Werfstrasse 5, Hamburg 11, Germany 2000

Stirling

ENERGY FOR SUSTAINABLE DEVELOPMENT LTD., 51 Artesian Road, London W2 5DB, UK

STIRLING DYNAMICS (P) LTD., 481 Mount Road, Nandanam, Madras 600 035, India

107

Annexe III   Glossary

active surface: the surface of the photovoltaic cell that faces the sun, where solar radiation is absorbed

angle of incidence: the angle between the incoming beam of solar radiation and an imaginary line perpendicular to the receiving surface

brushless d.c. motor: a direct current (d.c.) motor which uses electronic commutation to provide an alternating current (a.c.) for the field coils

coarse blade angles: windmill rotor blades which are angled away from the plane of the rotor to a relatively high degree. (A traditional Dutch windmill has coarse blades, but a modern wind generator does not)

commutator: part of a d.c. motor that switches the incoming d.c. electricity to a.c. electricity

critical month: the month in which the available wind energy is lowest relative to the energy that is required. This is the month for which the wind pump must be sized

deep cycle battery: a battery which can be electrically discharged to a greater degree than a normal battery

diode bridge: a device for converting a.c. electricity to d.c. electricity

electrodialysis: see **reverse-osmosis**

electronic commutation: the process of converting d.c. to a.c. for the brushless d.c. motor

flash evaporation: purification of water by a sudden reduction in pressure causing the water to evaporate, leaving impurities behind

groundwater contributions: water retained in the soil that contributes to crop growth

impedance matching: the process of matching the electrical load to a power source to allow the maximum transfer of power

kWe: kilowatts of electricity

kWpe: kilowatts of peak electricity

loss of prime: introduction of air into a pump which prevents the pumping of water

mini-grid: a local electrical grid for a town or village, which is independent of the country's national grid

national grid: a national network of electricity transmission lines

open-circuit voltage: the potential difference on a photovoltaic cell or array when no electrical load is connected

over-discharged: a battery that is electrically discharged beyond its recommended level for optimum life

potential difference: the voltage between two points in an electrical circuit

radio receiver: a radio or wireless

rainwater harvesting: collection of rainwater using, for example, roofs, sheets, canals and dykes

reverse-osmosis: the process of filtration of water by applying a pressure differential across a special membrane

slow sand filtration: filtering of water by forcing it through a sand bed

solar spectrum: the range of frequencies of electromagnetic waves received on the earth from the sun

spectral distribution: the intensity of solar radiation at different frequencies of the solar spectrum

thermosyphon: a system whereby water circulates without external pumping because of the density difference between hot and cold water

UHF transceiver: a radio receiver and transmitter operating on the Ultra High Frequency waveband

vapour compression: purification of water by compressing water vapour and using the heat generated to reduce external heating requirements